PARTY CONFIDENTIAL

new etiquette for fabulous entertaining

WRITTEN AND LIVED BY

lara shriftman and elizabeth harrison

with lara morgenson and elizabeth keen

ST. MARTIN'S PRESS ⚏ NEW YORK

PARTY CONFIDENTIAL: NEW ETIQUETTE FOR FABULOUS ENTERTAINING. Copyright © 2008 by Lara Shriftman and Elizabeth Harrison. All rights reserved. Printed in the United States of America. For information, address St. Martin's Press, 175 Fifth Avenue, New York, N.Y. 10010.

www.stmartins.com

Library of Congress Cataloging-in-Publication Data

Shriftman, Lara.
Party confidential : new etiquette for fabulous entertaining / Lara Shriftman and Elizabeth Harrison.—1st ed.
p.   cm
ISBN-13: 978-0-312-38211-7
ISBN-10: 0-312-38211-1
1.   Parties.   2.   Entertaining.   I.   Harrison, Elizabeth.   II. Title.
GV1471.S56 2008
793.2—dc22
2008007538

Book design by Charles Kreloff

First Edition: July 2008

10 9 8 7 6 5 4 3 2 1

CONTENTS

PARTY CONFIDENTIAL

THE STARTER COURSE
makin' a good first impression

MOVE OVER, MISS MANNERS! It's time to bring the fête-going and soiree-throwin' ladies and gents up to date on the yes and no ma'ams of party etiquette. The ugly truth is that everyone has sat down at a dinner party next to the good-looking guy who gabs with a mouthful of caviar. And don't even get us started about the designer-dressed dame who chows down with her elbows on the table. But these faux pas are elementary, my dear Watsons.

How do you handle last-minute invites? An unexpected guest? And what, God forbid, should you do if you spill a glass of '82 Lafite on an expensive white carpet? Relax, we've got the answers.

This modern-day guide is more than just a finishing school for social butterflies. As experts in our field, we've thrown countless parties (more than two hundred a year for the past fifteen years!) and as such, seen more gauche moves than we care to count. Some of Harrison & Shriftman's more fabulous events have included movie premieres for *Charlie's Angels, Bridget Jones Diary,* and *Legally Blonde;* store openings for Michael Kors, Jimmy Choo, Louis Vuitton, and Scoop; charity events for Love Heals and Toys for Tots; fashion shows for Catherine Malandrino, Oscar de la Renta, Jill Stuart, and Lacoste; product launches for BlackBerry, Cartier, Calvin Klein, Juicy Couture, and Motorola; birthday parties for Reggie Miller, Lara Flynn Boyle, Serena Williams, Luke Wilson, Paris Hilton, Stevie Wonder, and many, many more.

After penning the successful books *Fête Accompli!: The Ultimate Guide to Creative Entertaining* and *Party Confidential,* we found the recurring questions from friends, family, and members of the media were always about etiquette. How many people should be invited? Should we overinvite? How do you make sure everyone is going to show up for the party? How do you handle seating at a dinner? What do you do if someone had too much alcohol? What do you do if your caterer doesn't show up? What do you do if you run out of chairs or forget someone's place card? What kind of host gift should you bring? We get these questions—and more—every day. So when researching this book, we asked more than just the celebrities who live it up at splashy red carpet dos; we looked for advice from some of the premiere hosts and guests who get invited to every kind of shindig.

Because as times change, so do the age-old rules of misbehaving. In *Party Confidential: New Etiquette for Fabulous Entertaining,* we've taken a modernized approach to manners. We're not making up the rules; we're giving the old ones a "facelift." Social graces have gone through a major transformation since the days of Emily Post, so it's time for a book that addresses e-mail invites, cell phone texting, and the magical appearance of an unexpected (not to mention uninvited) guest of a guest. We've even narrowed down how to use those newfangled methods of meeting, like Facebook.

IT ALL BEGINS WITH THE BASICS IN CHAPTER ONE Party Planning 101. Simply put, people love parties, whether they are going or throwing one. But despite the fun factor associated with a fête, there is, on both sides of the list, the feeling of intimidation, dread, and nagging concerns. What if I wear the wrong thing? What if no one shows up? What happens if too many guests descend on my small garden party? Relax. Soirees are meant to be *fun.* Be creative, think out of the box—and above all, be organized! For example, feeling British? We've got the lowdown on putting together an afternoon tea from Jumeirah Essex House in New York.

IN CHAPTER TWO The Power Host, we help you brush up on your introduction skills, gracefully handle misbehavior, keep all hired waitstaff in line, and more. After we get you headed in the right direction, it's time to get into the nitty-gritty, like crafting the perfect invite—down to addressing the envelope—in chapter three: You're Invited. As for chapter four, Mind Your P's & Q's, well, that should explain it all! We'll turn you into an expert thank-you-note writer, explain how to accept a gift, and even show you the southern way of doing it up proper. Plus, leading designers Peter Som and Catherine Malandrino will help you land on the best-dressed list.

And that's just the tip of the ice sculpture. There's a myriad of other details like last-minute invitations, unexpected guests, and dealing with underperforming vendors. Experts in their fields lend you a helping hand, including Los Angeles doyenne Dani Janssen and Pink Taco owner Harry Morton, alongside insider tips from maître d's at top restaurants like Nobu, Koi, and Il Sole.

AND THE GUEST? Don't think for a moment there's not a code of conduct, just check out chapter five: Guestly Manners (we recommend you read it, reread it, and then read it once more!). We'll keep you at the top of everyone's list with our instructions. For example, that invite in the mail? Notice the last line, which says RSVP, and do it! Sending an e-mail saying you might attend if you feel like it is not an appropriate response. We'll crack the dress code, explain the parameters on arriving fashionably late versus just plain late, and show you how to pose like a red carpet pro with tips from photographers Tierney Gearon, Jeff Vespa, Patrick McMullan, and Myriam Santos-Kayda.

NEXT, IN CHAPTERS SIX AND SEVEN The Gallant Gourmet and Cocktail Conduct, you'll find integral advice on everything from providing proper bar service to setting a flawless table so you won't have to guess which side the wine glass goes on! Our finishing school wraps up with chapter eight, Get Toasted, where we make sure you'll never be at a loss for words again. We include the best glass-raising lines from your favorite Hollywood movies and celebrities Billy Bob Thornton, Sophia and Ava Schrager, Michael Michele, Molly Sims, Courteney and David Arquette, Hugh Jackman, Lara Flynn Boyle, and more.

AT A LOSS AS TO THE PERFECT HOSTESS GIFT? Look no farther than chapter nine: Present Perfect. Don't be the person who shows up with flowers or a green bean casserole ever again! We wrap it up by outlining the best gifts, when to bring them, and how to present them. You'll be the queen (or king) of presents!

AND AS A BONUS we've included our beloved Resource Guide, which is our yellow pages to throwing a fabulous bash. A must-have for a planner of any size party.

As entertaining experts, we've experienced all of these circumstances—and many more—and now we're imparting our social mores with all the humor we have left in us. Don't take our word as the final commandment; read, have fun, and adjust to what feels right to you. Party on, our well-mannered reader!

one

PARTY PLANNING 101

so, you wanna throw a party? here's how

IMAGINE THIS A gorgeous garden, twinkling with candlelight, and beautiful flowers blooming. Servers in white dresses circulate with trays of Champagne and delicious tidbits—like a sinfully delicious puff pastry stuffed with a smidge of cheese and charcuterie. Couples congregate on plush white sofas and sip cocktails by the bar while discussing the latest Britney Spears brouhaha and, wait, where did you get that dress? I must have it! As the evening charges on the tunes heat up and couples bounce onto the dance floor. Now that's a party.

SOUNDS AMAZING, RIGHT? Trust us, it is. Unfortunately, the mere thought of putting together even a cocktail party for the neighbors can put some hosts into a cold sweat. Relax, take a deep breath, and listen up. Throwing a bash is simple, easy, and most of all, fun, yes, fun! To illustrate the point, we've distilled the finer points of party planning into ten easy steps.

TEN NO-FAIL STEPS TO A FAB FÊTE

1. WHAT'S THE SCOOP? There are thousands of reasons to throw a party: a birthday, half-birthday, anniversary (wedding, one year since you quit smoking or kicked the coffee habit, lost twenty-five pounds, and so on), holiday (Halloween, Christmas, New Year's, Valentine's Day, Saint Patrick's Day, Memorial Day, Mother's Day, Father's Day, Fourth of July, Labor Day, Jewish New Year . . . there's even Columbus Day!), the summer solstice, winter solstice, upcoming wedding (engagement, bachelorette,

bridal shower), award-show viewing of any kind (Oscars, Emmys, Golden Globes, People's Choice, VH-1 Fashion Rocks, MTV VMAs, and more), a new job . . . any momentous occasion worth saying woo-hoo!

2. CONCEPT Pick a theme, whether it's a color or a full-on dress-up extravaganza, and go with it. Some of our favorites include: Leather and Lace, Golf Pros and Tennis Hos, Denim and Diamonds, CEOs and Secretary Hos, 70s, 80s, 90s, Dress as Your Favorite Celebrity, Barbie and Ken, Old Hollywood, Roller-Skating à la *Boogie Nights*, Beach Party, Vegas Casino Night . . . anything goes!

3. ORGANIZATION PLUS We can't emphasize this aspect more: the key to throwing any successful event is to be organized. Keep track of every single detail and we promise, your head won't implode! Create a master list that details each and every component, from the guest list to the vendors to the flowers.

4. THE GUEST LIST Before you can get the word out about your fabulous, not-to-be-missed event of the millennium, you have to decide who and how many to invite. Is this a small, intimate gathering? A big blowout? Do you need a host committee? If you have a guest of honor, be sure to discuss who they want in attendance. Mix it up; invite new acquaintances and old faves so guests extend their social network. And don't forget to overinvite! Out of every ten guests, plan on two no-shows. And always, always confirm guests. Not only does confirmation serve as a reminder to them, but ensures their attendance!

5. **MONEY TALKS** Okay, you know why you're partying and who you're inviting. Now you need to figure out how much you can afford to spend. Again, organization is important. Put together a dream list of everything you'll need to pull this baby off and then estimate how much it will cost, then add 10 percent. Also, when constructing your budget decide what is the most important aspect—is it invites or Cristal?

6. **SPOT ON** Location is everything! It could be your living room, backyard, the local park, the hottest new club in town, a swanky hotel suite, or a classic restaurant, like Mr. Chow, Dan Tana's, Hamburger Hamlet, or Cipriani's. Take into consideration how much space you'll need to accommodate the guest list and what your budget can handle. Be creative when choosing a location; think of a place where your guests will be delighted to spend the night.

7. **NEIGHBORHOOD WATCH** If you decide to throw your bash at home, there are some basic steps you won't want to forget. Namely, notifying the neighbors! The rebuffed girl-next-door could bring an end to your night, so let them know of your plans well in advance. Better yet, invite them over so they're a part of the merriment or send a fabulous gift beforehand to butter them up.

8. **THE A-TEAM** Make sure your staff knows what is expected of them. This includes hired staff (catering, valet, servers, cleaning, and more) as well as the staff at a location such as a restaurant or nightclub. If you're doing it at home, hiring help is still a must, even when you're strapped for cash (your nephew would kill for an extra fifty bucks, wouldn't he?).

9. GOOD VIBES You don't have to be a professional party planner to create a cool, interesting space. Think about your theme and what you can do to make it come to life. Consider the décor, lighting, music, and any extra-special touch that will make your gala the greatest ever.

10. LET THE GOOD TIMES ROLL Most important, make sure that you are enjoying yourself, because if you're not, you can be certain your guests aren't having any fun, either!

take note   Always use unscented candles at dinner parties; an overpowering scent can compete with the luscious smells coming from the prepared meal. Plus, you never know when a particular scent will turn a guest's stomach. At cocktail parties or any other kind of event, feel free to pick scented candles, but pick one single light fragrance and stick with it. Don't mix green tea candles with vanilla spice; separate they are lovely—but combined? Not so much!

WHAT MAKES A GOOD PARTY?

Ever wondered the secret of the best party in town? It certainly depends on the type of party you are throwing and who you are inviting. Take a tip from our hunky Hollywood men about town, Harry Morton and Hugh Jackman.

"Numero Uno. Hot girls. You can absolutely never have too many. Rule #2: Copious amounts of alcohol. You need to loosen everyone up. Rule #3: Amazing music. And last, top it off with flattering lighting. It can make a six look like a nine."

Harry Morton

"Having shots served to the guests at the door as they arrive."

Hugh Jackman

"People, music, food, and locale. All of the above should be great with preparation. The operative word is 'best.' The best of people, music, food, and locale."

Michael Michele

Take a tip from one of Hollywood's greatest hostesses, Dani Janssen, and make a sure statement about what you expect from your guests. This doyenne of Oscar night throws an annual after-party that is the most coveted invite in town. She crafts (and cooks!) a late-night dinner for Hollywood royalty like Jack Nicholson, Clint Eastwood, and Billy Bob Thornton. The day of her party she never answers the phone, which is her way of sending the no-cancellation message. In fact, to cancel, or worse yet, be a no-show, on this once-a-year event means you may be deleted from the list.

So how did Dani cultivate this implicit set of rules? It's simple—she creates a sensational evening and is tactfully honest about what she expects from her guests. Remember, it's your party, so you call the shots!

MUST DINNER PARTY INVITES BE RECIPROCATED?

As party planners, Lara and Elizabeth encounter this issue more times than they can count. They throw and attend countless parties, both business and personal. As a rule, you shouldn't expect a return invite unless you are going out of the way for a particular guest, perhaps by accommodating extra guests or something along those lines. If you're in a position to reciprocate an invite, consider the type of event you are planning. Is it big? small? intimate? Will the invitee mix with the guests you've already invited? If not, then wait for an appropriate occasion or take them out to lunch or dinner. Also, be aware of guests who invite you to an event because they want to attend your once-a-year Halloween Bash. If you don't want to feel beholden, then don't attend their party.

Bottom line, more important than responding with a return invite is responding with politeness; a handwritten thank-you card will do.

TEATIME

Afternoon tea is perfect for bridal and baby showers, birthday parties, Mother's Day, or whenever you're looking for an alternative to the cocktail party. This British custom dates back to the early 1800s, but the tradition gained popularity during Queen Victoria's reign and by the mid-nineteenth century, taking tea in the afternoon had become an established practice, with a complex set of rules and etiquette.

Needless to say, planning or attending an afternoon tea can be daunting, so to straighten out the confusion that often accompanies tea, we went straight to the authority, Christian Gradnitzer, executive chef at Jumeirah Essex House. This New York institution features homemade breads, scones, pastries, and sorbet alongside an assortment of loose-leaf black, green, herbal, and fruit teas. Tradition states that the proper way to take tea is to select from an assortment of finger sandwiches, followed by scones with jam and Devonshire clotted cream, and end with a selection of sweets. That being said, there are a slew of dos and don'ts when teatime rolls around. Gradnitzer lays down the law for the proper way of serving and taking tea.

for the guest

"Never hold your teacup with your pinkie finger extended. This is considered rude in most social settings. Place your index finger into the handle of the cup up to the knuckle while placing your thumb on the top of the handle to secure the cup. The bottom of the handle should then rest on your third finger. The fourth and fifth fingers should curve toward your wrist.

"Do not clink your spoon against the cup while stirring your tea. Swish the spoon gently back and forth without touching the sides of the cup. When done, remove the spoon and place it on the saucer behind the teacup. Remember not to drink your tea without removing the spoon from the cup and don't sip from the spoon.

"Do not lift the saucer, only the teacup. When you take a sip of tea do not look around at the other guests, but lower your eyes so you can see what you're doing and not spill your tea down the front of your blouse or dress.

"The correct manner in which one eats a scone is the same manner in which one eats a dinner roll. Simply break off a bite-size piece, place it on your plate, and then apply, with your bread and butter knife, the jam and cream.

"Be sure to take small bites, since attending a tea is a social occasion and you will want to participate in the conversation without always having a full mouth. Chew and swallow completely before taking a drink of tea, since it is hot and is not meant to wash the food down."

for the host

"Afternoon tea food placement for a three-tier stand: top tier for the scones; middle tier for the sandwiches; bottom tier, sweets. The protocol of placing the scones on the top tier is due to the fact that during the 1800s, when the genre of afternoon tea first became popular and modern kitchen conveniences did not exist, a warming dome was placed over the scones. The dome would only fit on the top tier. The savories and tea sandwiches, followed by the sweets, were placed on the middle and bottom tiers respectively.

"Offer a wide selection of teas to satisfy everyone's taste: black, white, green, oolong, or blended teas. Present the available teas in a beautiful wooden display box; guests can open the glass bottle to smell the aroma of the tea before selecting one.

"Change the afternoon tea 'theme' according to the season. For example, Jumeirah Essex House serves a refreshing lemon-themed afternoon tea during the hot summer months while during the colder months a holiday-themed gingerbread afternoon tea is served.

"Serve with appropriate afternoon tea china. The teapot is designed with a lower rounded body to ensure the tea leaves have the proper room for expansion during the infusion process. The lower placement of the spout on the vessel allows for the tea to be poured without interfering with the leaves. A teacup is shallow and wider than a coffee cup, giving the beverage a chance to temper before drinking.

"Using loose leaf teas allows greater flexibility, letting the guest brew weaker or stronger tea as desired. A strainer is used to avoid having to drink the floating loose leaves."

TIPS FIT FOR A BUNNY
BY MARY O'CONNOR

When it comes to parties and acting proper, there's one woman who's seen it all—and by all, we mean *everything*. Mary O'Connor, with the help of her team, has been running the ultimate Playboy's world from her position as Hugh Hefner's secretary/executive assistant for thirty-five years. O'Connor is the gatekeeper to the Playboy Mansion, home of the most-sought-after parties in all of Hollywood.

So no matter what kind of party you are planning, O'Connor has the insight to help you keep your playboys and girls feeling frisky!

how do you plan the guest list?

"Over the years we have built a list of five to six thousand people. That actually may be a low number. But we send out about twelve hundred invites."

how do you handle requests for invitations?

"They all fall into different categories. Young girls who've never attended a party are asked to submit a picture and a driver's license. We don't need underaged people drinking at the parties. You can look really hot when you're sixteen. That's one thing. Then the floods of pictures start coming. Agents, publicists, get wind and they all start calling."

what if a guy wants to come?

"It's much tougher for guys. It can't be an ordinary guy. It can't be a pharmacist or a doctor. He has to be some sort of celebrity. If he wants to bring a friend, it depends on the person. And people's status changes—it can go up or down. It is every guy's fantasy to go to a party at the Playboy Mansion."

what do you do when a guest brings an extra person?

"It depends. We've turned down celebs who have tried to sneak in extra guests in their car or even in their trunk. We've turned them away because if we don't stand our ground, we've lost."

how do you deal with bad behavior?

"Generally those people are escorted off the property. And how this is handled is important."

what about people who were out of line at a party and then want to be invited again?

"There is a fine line between getting into an argument, or saying 'We changed the list around, so it's not the same people. We want to give others a chance to come.' We try to finesse it that way."

what are your best party tips?

"Ambiance has a lot to do with it, as does the mix of a number of people. We like to serve grazing-type food, so people can eat while they drink."

what is your favorite party food?

"The best food is the food that keeps people moving. In other words, they can pick it up and move around, and a line doesn't queue up. All that said, the mansion is famous for its lamb chops. We do a thing with lamb chops that is like eating a lollipop—that is my favorite. We also have sushi, seafood, and all types of salads."

you have a lot of theme parties that are famous at the mansion—the pajama party, midsummer night's dream. tell us a bit about them.

"Theme is important with a party. You should always give people an idea of what they should wear. This past year we changed up the theme for a Midsummer Night's Dream. Hef decided it should be a Pirates of the Caribbean theme. Holly is a total Disney-ite. She loves everything Disney. Hef and Holly spent their sixth anniversary at the Disneyland Hotel in the Pirates of the Caribbean suite. For the first time we had outstanding male costumes. There was Captain Ahab, bare-chested guys, daggers, everything!"

how do you handle not dressing up?

"We don't allow them to come in. I take that back, it depends on who it is. If George Clooney came through the door and it was a sleep-wear theme, I'd have him take off his shirt and give him a bathrobe. If he was wearing a tux, I'd have him remove his tie. I would admit George Clooney."

what is your biggest party regret?

"A long time ago, which we regret to the hilt, was when Cameron Diaz was coming to the mansion. She is such a sweet and loving person and is so much fun at parties. She called and was with a major rock band that night. She asked if she could bring them to the party. Hef said she could bring two or three of the guys in the band, but not the whole group. Well, she never came and she's never been back to the mansion. This was a big mistake. We want Cameron Diaz as a friend. I know now that I can say 'bring it on.' They are who they are, and they are good for us."

what is your best party ever, and why?

"I think that it's the smaller parties. When I'm talking small, I'm talking about three to four hundred people. You aren't bombarded by people. It's overwhelming sometimes, and I can imagine what it's like for the celebs who are there.

"My favorite party at the mansion is the Fourth of July party. It's an all-day event with hot dogs, popcorn, swimming, and watching the girls play volleyball. We have a Dixieland marching band and fireworks. There are fifteen minutes of choreographed fireworks that make you glad you live in America."

what are the rules for the girls?

"There used to be a rule that the girls can bring their boyfriends around on New Year's Eve, because nobody wants to be alone on New Year's. Hef has eased up on the rule, and the girls he knows are allowed to bring dates to parties."

Mary O'Connor's Top Etiquette Tips

1. Always RSVP.

2. Don't bring a camera. Respect people's space and don't ask them to take pictures with you.

3. Don't smoke pot at parties. We follow the air, find it, and that person leaves. If they need to get high, they need to do it on their own turf.

4. Don't overdrink, and don't make us have to nurse you.

5. Be respectful of the property. People lose sight of the fact that this is somebody's home. Some people can be so full of themselves that they are rude to other guests, servers, and bartenders. You have to remember that you are an invited guest just like when you went to your grandmother's house.

RESTAURANT RULES

Hosting a party at a restaurant is one option because cooking, catering, cleaning, coat check, valet—all these details are handled. But you're not off the hook completely. There are major details to be addressed.

When choosing a restaurant or nightclub, we love to pick a place that is a classic spot—a place that people know and love. Alternatively, look for a hot new venue or go with the unexpected and choose a place that no one is familiar with to make your event stand out. Another great option is to choose an ethnic restaurant and make a theme of the evening. Go with Mexican, Chinese, Japanese, Italian, or any favorite food. Often this route can make the event cost a lot less than having it at a trendy A-list spot.

Whatever type of place you select, be sure to think about the mood of the party. Do you want high energy? Then go with a dinner club. In the mood for something intimate? Look for a restaurant with a private room. Once you've selected the location, you'll need to scout the lay of the land on a pre-party visit so you know exactly what to expect. Make note of anything you might want to supply, like specially created menus or flower arrangements.

If the restaurant is booked ask to put your name on the waiting list or to be notified if there is a cancellation. Without begging shamelessly (remember, flattery will get you everywhere), engage the reservations manager and explain why you want the reservation and how important the table is to you and your guests. Another approach is to enlist a friend or acquaintance who frequents the restaurant—connections darling, it's everything! If they have a good relationship with the establishment, ask that they make a phone call on your behalf.

take note   In addition to your waitstaff, be sure to tip the maître d' or host, valet, coat check, bartender, and anyone else who goes the extra mile to make your event enjoyable. For the waitstaff, the recommended tip is 15 to 20 percent, for exceptional service we suggest 25 to 30 percent. It's also especially considerate to write a thank-you note to those that went the extra mile. It'll make your next dinner a guaranteed success!

Table for Ten, Please!

- Make your reservation as far in advance as possible. The key to making your event successful is to establish a relationship with the person taking the reservation, whether it's the hostess, reservations manager, or owner.

- Be specific about the number of guests and the date and time of your party. Also, be sure to discuss in advance a preference for a specific table or location.

- Negotiate the menu and price beforehand. Not only does this simplify the bill but it also takes decision-making out of the hands of guests so they have more time to play!

- If you have a large group, consider signing a contract with the establishment in order to make sure everything is in writing and handled ahead of time.

- Provide the restaurant (including waitstaff, bartender, host, owner, and others) with a typed list of special requests. This includes items such as place cards, candles, cake, and so on.

- Always confirm your reservation two days before and again the day of the event.

- The day of the event you should arrive at least forty-five minutes before your guests to iron out last-minute details and bring additional items like gift bags, cake, centerpieces, etc. Inform the restaurant if you are running late—nothing spells disaster like a canceled reservation! If for any reason you must pull the plug on your party, don't forget to call the restaurant. Most high-end restaurants keep tabs on no-shows and no one wants to be on the blacklist!

take note   Be on top of the dress code. If you're not positive about
whether coats are required, call the restaurant ahead of
time so you can inform guests. No one wants to be the
guy wearing the ill-fitting, crest-blazoned jacket provided
by the maître d'!

bill bedlam

When picking up the tab, make advance arrangements, either by
handing over your credit card upon arrival, or negotiating an
agreed upon price and menu. Whichever route you take, just ensure
that no check is presented at the end of the meal. Don't forget to
discuss gratuity and ask that it be included in the total amount. If you
miss this step, make it a point to check the calculations to see if
gratuity is already included.

turning the tables

Though you called ahead of time, the host just seated you at a table
next to the kitchen door. You've been eyeing a plum table by the
window and the seat you've got is the last seat you wanted in the
house. What now?

First off, don't pout through your dinner. Politely ask the host if there
is another table where your party can be seated. Explain that you
really wanted that cozy booth or window perch in a sweet, soft
manner. Do not take attitude! Do not demand! That kind of attitude
may land you in the street. You might have to wait a bit longer for the
more desired location, but if it means that much to you, make it work.

The best plan of attack is to ask for a specific table when making your reservation.

Don't like the food? Be polite when sending it back! Don't throw your fork down in disgust and snarl—that's how you end up with a waiter or chef spitting in your meal! Simply call a server over and quietly explain that you ordered your salad with no tomatoes, the steak cooked rare, mushroom sauce on the side, or whatever is displeasing your palate.

gracious guest

At a party, it is important that guests be mindful of certain guidelines, both spoken and unspoken.

1. When you are seated, look at the menu right away and decide what you are going to order before chatting up your dining companions. If your host is footing the bill, avoid ordering the most expensive dish on the list. And remember, no one wants to sit next to a food critic, so keep your complaints to yourself!

2. RSVP! Respond promptly to the invitation and then show up on time.

3. Don't cancel at the last minute. If you absolutely must, be sure it's a solid reason. Cancellations are a sure-fire way to get your name at the top of the blacklist.

4. Don't ask if you can bring a date if the invite was addressed solely to you.

5. Don't drink—or eat—too much.

6. Don't move your place card or change your table assignment. The host seated you there for a reason, so go with it!

7. Never switch other people's seats. If there are empty seats, then fine, you can do so. Just check with the host first!

how to make a reservation

Now it's time to actually get a table at the hottest, hippest, or classiest place in town. We've asked for advice from the key holders at some of the hardest tickets in town: Corinne Lazarz, CFO Koi Restaurant Group; Wolfgang Puck, executive chef, Spago, Cut, Chinois, and others; Doug Major, general manager, Il Sole; Stephen Bruce, owner, Serendipity 3; Erika Matsunaga, general manager, Nobu; Michael Manoocheri, director of restaurant operations, Hotel Bel-Air; and Kerry Simon, chef/owner, Simon Kitchen LA and Las Vegas. You don't have to be a regular or a celebrity to get a reservation; it's about knowing how to work the scene. Lara suggests having someone from your office call and say, "I'm calling from Harrison & Shriftman to place a reservation for Thursday at nine p.m." This makes it sound like your company is a regular and it adds a little panache.

Here's what our experts say:

CORINNE LAZARZ "Before calling the restaurant know the amount of people, date, and time for your reservation. If you are flexible with dates and times have them ready before you call. Also try calling during nonservice hours, for example, not during lunch or dinner service. Plan ahead; most restaurants have a certain period they book out. If leaving a message, always repeat name and number."

WOLFGANG PUCK "Be polite on the phone and make reservations far in advance, especially in a popular restaurant."

DOUG MAJOR "Always be cordial. The host or hostess is your friend and actually wants to help you."

STEPHEN BRUCE "My top tips for reservation etiquette is to be prepared. Have all your information at hand and ready and treat the person taking the reservation with respect."

ERICKA MATSUNAGA "Please call as far in advance as possible. Please don't be afraid to place your name on the waiting list. We try to accommodate as many people as possible. Patience and flexibility are a plus."

MICHAEL MANOOCHERI "Be friendly, it may make the staff or reservationists more favorable when selecting your table!"

KERRY SIMON "Be overly polite when speaking to a reservationist, just as they are to you. Understand that most guests are all looking for the same time slots, especially when they have a show to catch after dinner. Name dropping can be extremely condescending. If you must drop an owner, chef, or manager's name, do it with sincerity: 'I'm a good friend of so and so, whatever you can do for me would be greatly appreciated, but if you can't accommodate us at that specific time, I completely understand.' This goes a long way. If you have given specific instructions upon making a reservation (special table, special occasion, vegetarian request, etc.), always end the conversation by asking the name of the reservationist. When staffers are asked for their name, it instills full accountability for your special requests—they've got your name!

what are your suggestions for tipping the maître d' or hostess?

People are always intimidated by tipping, but these handy suggestions from those in-the-know take the guesswork out of the dollar.

WOLFGANG PUCK "Never tip before you are at the table. Tip on the way out."

ERICKA MATSUNAGA "Offering money at the door is offensive and ineffective. Remember that tips are a sign of appreciation."

MICHAEL MANOOCHERI "Matter of personal opinion. I feel it is unnecessary unless the person goes above and beyond."

STEPHEN BRUCE "Only tip the maître d' or hostess if you received exemplary service."

KERRY SIMON "A maître d' is somewhat of a thing from the past. However, they are still utilized in older establishments that cater to the older clientele. In today's modern restaurants, it is not required to tip 'the door' unless they have gone out of their way or job scope to fulfill a special request. In most restaurants today, the servers tip the door to ensure proper seating rotation and flow."

what are your tips for canceling a reservation?

Everyone always has that day when an emergency or something unexpected throws a wrench in the plans. Whether it's a fender bender on the way to dinner or the attack of a killer flu, sometimes things just don't go your way. But you can't just let that table for twelve sit empty all night. Here's how the pros suggest you call the whole thing off.

DOUG MAJOR "Always call and cancel to give the host or hostess an opportunity to rebook the table. Call even if it is ten minutes before your arrival time."

WOLFGANG PUCK "Cancel as soon as you know you cannot make it."

STEPHEN BRUCE "Always call as soon as you know you cannot make your reserved time. If you are stuck somewhere and late, call to inform the restaurant. No-shows are definitely frowned upon and remembered, so always inform a restaurant if you are not coming."

ERICKA MATSUNAGA "Please call. Cancellation is always better than a no-show so we can accommodate somebody else from the waiting list."

MICHAEL MANOOCHERI "Always call to cancel. Call well in advance when possible; make sure to ask about any cancellation fees or policies."

KERRY SIMON "Always give as much notice as possible. Many people will make multiple reservations in town in order to have several choices once they've gathered their group. This is fine, except when they rudely fail to cancel the others. Ever wonder why so many restaurants these days require credit card deposits for large parties? Now you know. No-shows result in not only the restaurant losing money, but also the tipped server, who was relying on the sales."

how to avoid waiting for a table

Everyone waits. It doesn't matter who you are or how often you eat at a particular place, there are things that are out of your control. Restaurants overbook (especially those that are in high demand), and people linger over their dessert and loiter over their last sip of wine for what feels like an eternity. Don't be the grumpy Gus, follow the maître d' protocol.

MICHAEL MANOOCHERI "Arrive early, confirm the reservation in advance; book outside of peak periods."

WOLFGANG PUCK "Be courteous."

CORINNE LAZARZ "Check in on time or slightly early with the host and don't demand a particular table. Also, make reservations earlier since they have first seating and it's usually less busy."

KERRY SIMON "Ever been told 'we don't have anything available until later' yet the room has a great deal of empty tables? Makes you think you're getting the ol' brush off. Not the case. Most dining experiences are roughly ninety minutes long. The tables that you see empty are already earmarked for reservations arriving within a certain time frame. At the beginning of the night, the floor is 'mapped out' to ensure each reservation is covered. This all said, don't be frustrated with watching empty tables go unseated for long periods of time. If 'the door' does not hold a specific number to cover their reservations, they will be in big trouble explaining to the guest with the reservation why they don't have it ready."

how to get the best table in the house

Got your eye on that perfect table situated in that oh-so-desirable location, maybe a cozy booth tucked in a private corner (perfect for that tête-a-tête with Mr. Big) or the see-and-be-seen table in the center of the action. These tips will ensure you get your spot!

MICHAEL MANOOCHERI "Ask for it when making the reservation. Be a loyal and frequent client."

WOLFGANG PUCK "Call as far ahead as possible and be friendly and polite."

CORINNE LAZARZ "You should have a better pick at tables if you book your reservation at the first available seating. If you have a particular table in mind, put the request in at the time of the reservation."

KERRY SIMON "If you reach a voice mail system during nonoperational hours and need to leave a message, always speak slowly, spell out your name, and leave your cell number, not your home or office number. If your guest count changes be sure to call and confirm the new count. Many parties drop in numbers and fail to inform the restaurant until they arrive. Empty seats will only aggravate the server who could have used them otherwise."

two

THE POWER HOST

the hostess with the mostes'

THE BIG NIGHT HAS FINALLY ARRIVED You're rushing around the house adjusting floral arrangements, lighting candles, giving last-minute instructions to staff, and taking one last peek in the mirror to make sure you look gorgeous (and naturally, you do).

But it's more than the décor and passed appetizers that make a gathering successful—the final ingredient is you: the host. As the chief of the festivities there are a thousand and one details that will need your attention throughout the course of the night: Are the guests mingling? Do they need cocktails? Is that guy drinking too much? Did you unwittingly invite two archenemies? Things can get hairy and the last thing you want is to have the night end in some sort of *Dynasty*-like pool plundering hair-pulling scene.

ENTER THE POWER HOSTESS The pointers in this chapter will give you the tools to handle any and every situation with grace. We outline everything from how to deal with smokers and uninvited guests to tipping the staff and getting out a stain. Finesse, charm, and attention to detail—that's the power host. That's you.

POWER MOVES: TEN THINGS EVERY HOST SHOULD DO

What makes a perfect host? These tips will make you the toast of the town.

1. RELAX AND ENJOY! If you don't have a good time at your own party no one else will!

2. DON'T DO IT ALONE Enlist a co-host (or two, three, or as many as you need), be it your husband, boyfriend, best friend, co-worker, mother, or anyone with whom you team up well. If your best bud, love her dearly, is flaky and disorganized, then don't ask her to be your co-host. If you ask her anyway, just be aware of her strengths and weaknesses and plan accordingly. Look for someone who can manage details and will happily step in during the messiest of moments.

3. BE READY AT LEAST FORTY-FIVE MINUTES BEFORE THE SCHEDULED START OF THE PARTY This gives you time to relax and wind down before guests arrive. There's nothing worse than being the first person to arrive only to find the host in the bathroom applying makeup or running around the house fretting over unlit candles and chair arrangements.

4. KNOW YOUR GUESTS The best way to be prepared is to know about those attending. The better you know your guests, the better you can anticipate what will make the night more

enjoyable for them. Do they drink? Does everyone like each other? Will they want to bring a guest? For example, if you know that since the invites went out, Paris and Nicole are, once again, on the outs, then you'll be able to avoid conflict by rearranging the table seating to put as much distance between the two as possible. And if you are having a dinner party, you should always be aware of any dietary restrictions guests may have, kosher, vegan, diabetic, and make arrangements ahead of time.

5.   EVEN STEVENS One of the most important parts of being a host is crafting the perfect guest list. The right mix of people is what makes a party great. There's nothing worse than being a single girl in a sea of couples. Where's the fun and flirting in that? So keep it equal and balance the number of men and women, singles and couples, gay and straight. Play your invites right and you just might become known for making matches!

6.   THINK OF THE LITTLE THINGS THAT WILL MAKE GUESTS FEEL WELCOME AND COMFORTABLE For example, if the weather turns chilly during your backyard barbecue, offer warm socks for those in sandals, a sweater or coverup to someone with bare shoulders, or if you have heat lamps on hand, crank up the temperature!

7.   COCKTAILS=WELCOME The minute guests arrive offer to get them a drink or better yet, have a tray of drinks at the door so they immediately feel like they are a part of the party. And they won't have to dash to the bar straight away.

8. MAKE INTRODUCTIONS Personally take guests by the hand and introduce them to as many people as you can. Getting guests to mingle is your responsibility, especially at the outset. We always suggest giving "introducees" seeds of conversation before leaving them alone to fend for themselves. Find their common ground to get the conversation flowing. "Fred, this is Mindy, she's the head of HSN. You should tell her all about your new line!"

9. MIX 'N' MINGLE Don't spend your night in the kitchen or handing out instructions to the help. Tell your waitstaff everything ahead of time, or better yet, write it all out and post it so they won't interrupt you with questions. Now you have time to circulate through the room, to talk to each and every guest, and to make new introductions! The more you move from conversation to conversation, the more your guests will.

10. BREAK THE ICE! Find creative ways to get your guests to interact: have a bunch of Polaroid cameras on hand, make people move around for each course at a seated meal, or put questions on their place cards. Inducing repartee isn't as tricky as it sounds. Invest in cool conversation starters like Table Topics. These cards feature fun, topic-inducing questions and they really work! They produce more interesting conversation than you'd dare try to create.

AVA AND SOPHIA SCHRAGER'S PARTY TIPS FOR THE ULTIMATE KIDS' PARTIES

Ava and Sophia Schrager are two of Lara's best friends. She has thrown them countless parties, and they have attended so many of her own bashes. Ava and Sophia, though only ten and thirteen years old, respectively, always give Lara and Elizabeth the best and most creative ideas. These two girls throw amazing, buzz-inducing parties that all of their friends love attending! These girls are the authority on kids' parties, having thrown everything from a Roller Disco Birthday Bash to Sophia's annual Halloween party. And there's nothing better than to get tips from young people who are out there in the field doing it their way—and the right way—and applying the ideas to parties for adults.

1. You need to have a great theme and make sure you have great decorations and food.

2. If you want to have a smaller party, that's fine, just be selective and make sure nobody feels left out.

3. Mixing different groups of friends at a party is good, but make sure you personally walk people around and introduce them.

4. If you're inviting one person who doesn't know anybody else in the group, invite them with a friend so they feel more comfortable.

5. For smaller parties, try to keep the number of men and women even so nobody feels outnumbered.

6. When you're planning a party, and picking your date, make sure nobody else is having a party that weekend. You can't have your party the day before a friend's party. Everyone will be tired, and you don't want to do that to your friend.

7. If you're having a party that happens to fall on someone else's birthday, you have to acknowledge your friend's birthday. The hostess should get up on the mic, announce the friend's birthday, and even sing "Happy Birthday." Sophia has been to parties where the hostess brought a cupcake for the birthday girl. You have to share!

if someone you know is already having a holiday party, would you have one?

"If it's just a few girls, sure. I'm known for having a huge Halloween party, so nobody else has a Halloween party. But if someone knows you have an annual holiday party, and they have one as well, you make sure that yours is bigger and better than theirs."

how do you handle inviting adults and kids to the same party?

"First, you must always invite the party planner. You can invite a few cool adults that you know and like, then it's up to your parents as to which parents they want to invite. Like my mom will say, 'Let's invite so-and-so, she'd be a fun adult to hang out with at the party.' If it's a kids' party, I don't mind adults, but some of my friends may hesitate to have a good time and dance when adults are around. You just want to be careful to make sure you don't let the adults make the kids feel like they can't have a good time."

how do you get boys and girls to mingle at the parties? what if there's that girl and she's left out from dancing? how do you handle this?

"I'm at that point right now that girls and boys are friends, so they hang out. At Bat Mitzvahs I've seen girls even dance with their fathers after the father/daughter dance. I've seen parties have motivational dancers who get everyone to dance. You can approach wallflowers and say, 'Come on, come dance.' After a while, what can you do? All you can do is try to make sure everyone is having a good time."

smaller parties versus big parties—when is it okay to just invite your best friends?

"On your actual birthday, you can pick a few of your best friends and invite them to a nice dinner. Save the big party for another night."

chic tip

Remember, entertaining should be fun—not the stuff that leaves you sweating bullets in the middle of the night. The key to being a great host is to make your party a natural extension of you. Don't make a seven-course home-cooked meal if the only thing you know how to do is order in! If you want to give a dinner party and your chef skills leave something to be desired, then reserve a private room at your favorite restaurant. A party should be a celebration of what you and your friends love!

take note

Always overinvite and overconfirm. Be prepared, because people will cancel at the last minute! Sending out the invitation is only the first step. Chances are you will have a couple of invitees who don't RSVP. Be prepared to tap into your B-list and know how to do it without them knowing you are doing this.

SHORT NOTICE

This is never an easy task because the last-minute invite has the potential to offend. But a wonderfully mannered host (like yourself) knows how to extend even a last-minute invite with ease. And let's face it, if you're planning a small dinner party and three people cancel, why waste the food? Cancellations happen, whether it's due to a crisis at work or home, or something happened en route, and a fantastic hostess can pick up the phone and fill those empty chairs.

But how? Foremost, anticipate cancellations. They will almost always happen, so plan your approach. There's the honest Abe approach and the little white lie. Let's face it, there are those who will be offended for not being on the list from the beginning, and in that case . . . stretch the truth. Just an itsy bit.

- **Be honest** Reach out to your spontaneous pals and lay it all out: "I realize this is short notice, but I made dinner for a few friends. I would absolutely love if you would join us." Don't apologize or make a huge deal out of the fact that they weren't invited in the beginning; instead, emphasize how happy you'd be to have Sally be a part of the evening. If it's a small, intimate gathering this is absolutely the best approach.

- **You forgot** Yes, there are cases where a white lie is the better approach. "I'm so embarrassed because I thought I had contacted you about my party tonight! Please tell me you can make it despite my oversight!"

- **Invite returned in mail** You know that stack of mail that piles up on your desk? Here's where it comes in handy. Simply confess that you hadn't paid a bit of attention to your incoming letters and did not see that theirs had been returned unopened. Be sure to verify their address so it won't happen next time!

- **RSVP to the rescue** This method is best applied when it's a large guest list. Simply call Ryan and say that you are getting a head count for tonight's bash and you noticed you hadn't heard back from him; is he planning to attend?

chic tip

The day of the party call all the guests on your list to confirm they will be there; plus, your call serves as a reminder for those who might be a bit on the forgetful side. This is especially important if you are having a small, intimate function like a luncheon or dinner party where guests will be seated. And if you're running short pull out the B-list and start the last-minute invite song and dance.

take note

Most people think a gift bag is required of a good host, but it's not a must. You are welcome to provide a little something for your guests if you so desire, maybe a box of sweets or something homemade. Dani Janssen always sends her guests home with a brown paper bag, marked with their name and filled with their favorite food. Now that's a gift worth giving!

DIFFUSING DISASTERS

A good host can handle any party catastrophe with ease. Toilets overflow, guests get drunk, spills happen . . . what else can possibly go wrong? This is the area that makes or breaks a host. We've rounded up some of the biggest party offenders and found a way to make them nothing more than spilt milk.

p r o b l e m   **Crisis! You have to cancel.** Emergencies happen for hosts as well as guests and there may come a time when you have to call off the big night or change the date. What now?

s o l u t i o n   **Organization, it's a plus!** The key is to get the ball rolling as soon as you realize the date must be changed or event canceled. This is when painstaking organization comes into play. When planning your party keep everyone's contact information easily accessible and clearly listed. Make an Excel spreadsheet, keep a binder—whatever works for you. Just be sure it includes contact information for the guests and all the help. Enlist your co-host and start dialing.

Don't e-mail! Try to talk to each individual personally unless you know it's someone who's always on their BlackBerry or e-mail and will see your note. Make the calls short 'n' sweet, as you don't have time to find out that Beth just started dating Sam, Denise's ex.

p r o b l e m   **Guests won't go home.** You've dismissed the staff but there's still die-hard stragglers hanging out on the back porch drinking and smoking or maybe there's a newly formed couple that just isn't ready to call the night quits. Meanwhile, you can barely keep your eyelids open and all you want to do is crawl in bed.

s o l u t i o n   **Show them the door!** Courtney Love's method of ending an evening is to take off her makeup and put on her bathrobe. Hey, who said you had to be subtle?

- Raise the lights and turn the music off. A great way to give guests a hint is to start playing mellow, ambient tunes about thirty minutes to an hour before you'd like the party to end. Party-goers will feel the switch in the vibe, and hopefully take the hint. If not, kill the tunes and bring on the brights!

* Politely ask the lounging lingerers to leave. Simply say, "I'm beat and it's been a long night!"

* Still not getting the hint? Go to bed! Turn off the lights, close your door, and crawl into your 1,000 thread count of bliss.

p r o b l e m **How do you handle gifts** of food, flowers, wine, or alcohol that you don't want to display or serve?

s o l u t i o n **People like to arrive** at a dinner or cocktail party with a bottle of wine in hand, but personally, Lara likes to send it before or after the dinner. Of course, it also depends on the type of event you are attending and how well you know the host. If the host knows you are bringing dessert or has asked you to make your famous upside-down chocolate banana pie, then by all means, start cooking! But if you bring something unannounced, be aware that the host might not want to serve it, as much as he or she appreciates your thoughtfulness. Perhaps they've planned something specific like a wine-paired dinner or an all-chocolate dessert bar. So when you arrive with a gift in hand, make it clear that you don't expect it to be served. "These are my special peanut butter cup cookies, you can serve them tonight—or keep them all to yourself!" Same goes with flowers. "I picked these up for you because I thought they were beautiful. If you'd like to tuck them away, I completely understand!" And the same goes for the host. If you receive something that doesn't fit with the event planned, simply thank the giver profusely and add with a wink, "I'll keep this all to myself!"

problem **Dealing with smokers.** Sally McSmokey plows through a pack of cigarettes in a matter of minutes—or so it seems. And now she's lighting up in the middle of your cocktail party and people are shooting her dirty looks.

solution **Extinguish the cigarette.** Drinking and smoking often go hand in hand, so establish the rules of smoking upfront. Decide beforehand with your co-host who will handle the smoky situations, so if someone lights up in a "restricted" area, it's immediately handled.

- Don't hesitate to ask someone to step outside or put out their cigarette. Remember, being a good host doesn't mean letting guests run wild and do as they please.

- Create a designated smoking area: set up ashtrays on the back patio, front porch, or wherever you are comfortable with cigarette smoke. If you're fine with smoking in the house, you still need to designate an area, as not all guests are comfortable with smoke in their eyes.

- Don't put ashtrays anywhere other than the smoking area (or don't put out at all if you prefer a nonsmoking environment).

- Ask the waitstaff to remind smokers that no one is to smoke inside.

- If someone continually gets up during dinner to smoke, you may ask them politely to refrain until the end of the meal or to only do so between courses. Guests should also note, if you are a smoker, try to refrain from lighting up during dinner. At the end of the dinner, excuse yourself and head outside to get your fix.

p r o b l e m **Fight! Fight!** Uh, oh, here comes trouble. Paris and Nicole may be friends now, but that wasn't the case two years ago. But the two girls still showed up at the same events and the tension could be cut with a knife.

s o l u t i o n **Overruled!** Establish order and most important, know your guests. If you're planning a small, intimate dinner, then don't invite people who openly dislike each other. If it's a huge gala and you absolutely want the warring parties present then be upfront and let each one know the other will be there. Ask them to refrain from crossing paths out of respect for you.

If conflict does arise, whether two testosterone-fueled males decide to be Mr. Macho Men and throw punches or a couple of mouthy babes start shrieking at one another, immediately call a cease fire and ask them to take it outside, away from your guests. Do not allow this to become an interruption and spoil everyone's evening.

p r o b l e m **Imposing guests.** They arrive with an entourage, they call and ask to bring a first date to your sit-down luncheon for ten, or they just arrive at your dinner party with an extra person in tow.

s o l u t i o n **It's your party, don't cry.** How you handle guests that impose varies from party to party and how it affects you. Do you like the extra guest (or ten) that Tom just brought? How big is the party? If it's a large gathering, the best approach is to just let it go. But if space is an issue, like at a seated event, there are a few ways to overcome this obstacle.

- At a dinner party, squeeze in an extra chair next to Tom, who brought his new girlfriend. If you only have ten cornish game hens and are now eleven, simply divide Tom's dinner in half and tell him, "You won't mind sharing, will you?" It's the perfect way to get the message across without making everyone at the table squirm.

- If someone calls up prior to the party and asks to bring an uninvited guest, the decision is completely yours. Do you like the person? Are you able to accommodate another body? You have the right to say no (and while you're at it, buy Tom a copy of this book with the chapter on guest etiquette bookmarked!).

- If you're wavering, go the route that Patrick McMullan refers to as "toothpick guests." Just invite Tom's guest to cocktail hour or have him/her come after dinner and join everyone for dessert.

- And guests of guests? Not allowed! Apologize for not being able to accommodate the extra individual and let them know you'd be happy to have them return another time. Politely ask the invited guest to explain the situation to his entourage and let him handle the uncomfortable moment.

problem **Too many people!** The place is packed and there's barely room to squeeze past the couch in order to reach the bar.

solution **Grin and bear it.** After all, it's the price you pay for being the most popular host in town! If you follow the golden rule and plan for overages, then you won't have to worry when everyone you invited shows up. Of course, both hosts and guests should know how to navigate a crowded room. First tip: Don't order a martini! If elbow room is at a premium, it's only a matter of time before your pink cosmo splashes on someone's brand-new Birkin bag. If you must have your drink shaken and not stirred, forgo tradition and ask for it to be served in a highball glass. Second, carve out a space and stay there! And last, say excuse me as you shuck and dive through the masses of people. Politeness goes a long way in forming a path!

problem **Bedroom butt-ins.** You didn't need to see that! You ran back to your bedroom to switch shoes or do a quick touchup only to find two sweaty lovers embracing on your bed. Yikes!

solution **Get a room,** seriously. First of all, let's hope your party-going friends would know better. But maybe the connection is just too hot to make it home. Whatever the case, you have two choices: ask them to get dressed and move the love show elsewhere or close the door and walk away. If you choose the latter, why not get in a zinger like, "Can you please change the sheets when you're done? The linen closet is in the hall." That should get the message across!

problem **Bathroom bust-ups.** There's nothing worse than an out-of-service bathroom. Too much toilet paper, too many people, and things can get ugly. Fast.

s o l u t i o n **Roto-Rooter, anyone?** Pray you have another bathroom! If that's not the case, it's time to get messy. Be sure to post a sign on the door that informs guests that the bathroom is not to be used and then get to work.

- If you know you have fussy plumbing, consider getting the lines snaked prior to your big event or, better yet, for large events consider renting a portable restroom.

- Always have a plunger on hand and the number of a twenty-four-hour plumber or handyman who you know will be there faster than the speed of light.

chic tip   The bathroom is the one place in your home guests are guaranteed to visit, so make it pleasant! Keep the lights dim and light a candle. Be sure to have plenty of toilet paper and guest towels on hand and a bowl of mints on the vanity. You may also choose to have a bottle of hair spray on hand for touchups as well as a pleasantly scented lotion. And if you only have one bathroom, dissuade guests from lingering!

p r o b l e m **Supplies run dry.** Nothing breaks up a fun night faster than running out of the bare necessities like ice and toilet paper. To ensure this doesn't happen, always, always overbudget and buy more than you think you will need. Unfortunately . . . this time you didn't. Don't let people start inventing new ways to wipe—let's not even think about where that hand-stitched guest towel might go!

s o l u t i o n **Beer run!** Grab the keys and have your co-host, one of the waitstaff, servers, or any spare help (be sure to slip them a few extra dollars for their time) rush off to the nearest grocery or convenience store. Keep a list of places on hand that deliver for such emergencies, but the best advice is to buy twice as much as you think you will need. But if you run out, whether it's a mixer or a party necessity like ice, don't grin and bear it, go get it!

p r o b l e m **Neighbor complaints.** Nosy Nancy next door is never happy and has the police department on speed dial. The last party you had ended with the cops knocking on the door at 9 p.m. asking you to turn the music off and get the cars out of the street.

s o l u t i o n **Silence 'em with kindness.** Nip that situation in the bud by keeping your neighbors in the loop. Don't throw a two-hundred-person party complete with valet and a live band without warning your neighbors. But there are a few things that can make the family next door a bit more amiable—and we're not just talking about earplugs.

- Invite them! Make them a part of the party and they won't have a reason to complain.

- Send flowers or Champagne before the big night with a note thanking them for their understanding.

- Don't overdo it. If you have a big blowout every month you will be on the neighborhood blacklist. One a year for a special occasion or just keep 'em small.

problem **Weather won't cooperate.** You've spent weeks planning your beachside clambake, it's the middle of June, and the temperature hasn't dipped below 90 degrees in weeks. Now suddenly, the night is here and of all things, the heat has broken the night of your party. Guests are freezing and you don't have any heat lamps!

solution **This actually happened** recently when Lara threw a dinner party at her Malibu beach house. Los Angeles had been suffering (yes, suffering) from 100 degree heat and the nights had been hot and sticky. So she didn't order heat lamps. Hosts should keep cozy blankets, shawls, or sweaters so chilly guests can warm up. If you can move the party inside, do so, otherwise, get out those sweatshirts and blankets and get the hot chocolate boiling!

HEY, DADDY BIGBUCKS! CAN YOU SPARE A DOLLAR?

Whether you throw your party in your smashing abode or the latest hotspot, the end of the night brings out the wallet. Bartenders, servers, housekeeping, valet, catering—they all expect to be rewarded for their work. Remember, the key to having excellent help is to reward them accordingly. A bartender will happily agree to work your next party if you hand him an envelope on his way out.

Remember, tips add up quickly and depending on the cost of your party can easily add up to a few thousand dollars, so be sure to factor this extra expense into your budget. And of course, you need to know who to tip and when the right moment is to slip them some extra dollars.

Restaurants and clubs often factor gratuity into the bill, so be sure to check the total carefully. In addition, keep in mind that a follow-up thank-you note and recommendation are often a valued tip as well. But when it comes to the bottom dollar, how much is just right? Who gets an envelope of green and who doesn't? Commit this chart to memory, make a copy, rip it out, and before you know it every starving actor will be clamoring to work your glamorous gala. Be sure to put tips in an envelope for each recipient and hand them out at the end of the night after the guests have gone and their work is complete.

While the tip chart on the following page is a handy resource, you should keep in mind where you are having the party and how many people are at the party. If the individual went above and beyond, we highly recommend you reward by overtipping.

take note

Yes, tip jars serve a purpose in reminding guests that the coat check, bathroom attendant, valet, and bartender need a little somethin' somethin'. But Lara is not a proponent of the tip jar, mainly because they look tacky. It's up to each guest to decide whether or not they want to tip, and they shouldn't be made to feel that it is their responsibility. It is the host's concern, so plan on handing out an envelope to the staff members who have interacted with guests at the end of the night. This also allows you to give extra to those who went above and beyond the call of duty.

Don't Be a Cheapo

VENDOR	AMOUNT
Catering Staff	15 to 25 percent of total bill
Banquet Manager	$100 to $200
Chefs	$50 each
Wait and Kitchen Staff	$20 to $30 each (depends on how long and how many people worked, how many guests they served, five or five thousand; gauge 15 to 25 percent of your event cost)
Housekeeping	$20
Bartender	15 to 25 percent of total bill (for a party, that would be the bar total)
Valet	$2 per vehicle (estimated by number of guests attending). If guests are paying the valet, you can slip them anywhere from $20 to 100, depending on the number of cars.
Bathroom Attendants	$1 to $2 per attendant
Coat Check	$2

Note: Many companies include gratuity in the contract and then divide it among their workers, so when negotiating the contract be sure to ask if gratuity is included in the quote. You may also offer a flat amount as specified above.

An excellent host always thinks of the little things. Tip the valet at the beginning of the night and have him inform guests intending to tip that tipping has already been taken care of. In addition, have the drivers leave a bottle of water or a single flower in each car.

ON THE SPOT

Spills happen. Cabernet Sauvignon splotches, soy sauce splashes, cranberry 'n' vodka dribbles, chocolate mousse smears . . . oh, just think of the havoc one night can wreak upon a plush white interior! Of course, there are those who circumvent these horrors by serving only clear-colored drinks (we're not sure if they draw the same line when it comes to food), but sooner or later, a spot is bound to rear its ugly head. Nip this party pooper in the bud by always having an arsenal of stain removers on hand.

problem **Spills!**

solution The proper plan of attack combined with our must-have arsenal can ensure a spill won't permanently dirty your reputation. Keep as many as possible of these stain-removal products on hand.

* Oil Solvents (K2R or Carbona—found at any local drugstore. Carbona has a convenient stain roller with roller head that dispenses an all-natural cleaner for five bucks.)

- Combination solvents (Shout or Spray 'n Wash). Shout makes handy, individually wrapped wipes perfect for concentrated application on small stains. Added bonus: wipes are priced under three bucks.

- Digestants (we like BIZ)

- Absorbents (talcum powder)—perfect for oily/greasy stains

- Bleaches (the mainstay—Clorox). Make your own bleach substitute with white vinegar or lemon juice diluted with one part water. Make sure the bleach only goes on the stain (use a Q-Tip for focused application).

- Spray Febreze on your couches to rid them of the smell of smoke and last night's bash. Open up the windows, light some candles . . . et voilà!

- Detergent or soap (use a translucent liquid detergent like Dawn or Joy)

- Glycerine is especially effective on ballpoint pen stains

adhere to these basics of stain removal

- Act as quickly as possible. As soon as a spill occurs, blot up as much as possible with an absorbent cloth or paper towel (use a white cloth or paper towels with no prints).

- Always use cold water on a fresh stain.

- Blot—don't rub! Rubbing can spread the stain or cause it to set deeper. Instead, gently blot stain, working from the outside in.

- Do a spot test! Before treating the area with any solvent or cleaning product, always spot-test on an inconspicuous area of the carpet/upholstery.

misfired merlot? try these easy home remedies to treat the ever-dreaded red wine stain

- Salt! Pour salt on a fresh stain to absorb excess liquid.

- Mix three parts baking soda with one part water. Apply to stain. Let dry and vacuum.

- Shaving cream. A dab of foaming shaving cream has been shown to be effective in treating red wine stains.

take note If you have an all-white house, it's acceptable to serve only clear liquids like white wine, vodka, and gin with uncolored mixers (such as tonic and soda water). It lessens the stress for all parties involved!

carpets

Use the formulas in the chart that follows to ensure that you are using the best possible remedy for your type of carpeting. Pour the solvent into a spray bottle and mist lightly onto the stain.

	SYNTHETIC CARPETS	NATURAL FIBER CARPETS
The Detergent Solution	Mix ¼ teaspoon translucent liquid detergent (Dawn or Joy) and 1 cup lukewarm water	Mix 1 teaspoon of translucent liquid detergent (Dawn or Joy) and 1 cup lukewarm water
The Vinegar Solution	Mix 1 cup white vinegar with 2 cups water	Mix ¼ cup white vinegar with ¼ cup water
The Ammonia Solution		Mix 1 tablespoon clear household ammonia with ½ cup lukewarm water

 Use an emery board to remove small stains from suede or leather! Gently rub the file (either side) across the problem area. Do not use ammonia-based sprays on pet accidents. Urine has an ammonia-like odor that may bring Fido back for round two.

WHAT IS YOUR PARTY NIGHTMARE?

Every host has something that keeps them tossing and turning the night before the big event. Perhaps it's the fear of running out of ice, or that no one will come, or worse yet, no one will mingle! Here's what keeps our favorite hosts biting their nails through the eleventh hour.

"Creating a beautiful, elegant, classy evening and someone arrives as though it's going to be a frat house, crazy celebration. Loud, obnoxious people are my worst nightmare."

Michael Michele

"A woman walked into my home and went to the terrace to fawn over a celebrity friend. When they came into the living room, I thought he looked uncomfortable and not recognizing her, I went over to ask who she was with. She told me she was a countess and didn't have to be with anyone. I grabbed her arm, pulled her away from my friend, and said, 'I don't care if you're the queen,' and threw her out the front door. The next day I found out she really was a countess who was attending a party on the floor below mine."   Dani Janssen

"Running out of alcohol is the absolute worst."

Hugh Jackman

HOW TO AVOID OVERINVITING

Striking the perfect balance of invited guests can be tough. You don't want too many, you don't want too few. But you have to overinvite because a lot of times people who are invited don't come, people have things come up, they go out of town, they get sick, things come up at work or home, and so on. Expect right off the bat for two-thirds of the people you invite to send a regret, so think about that when drawing up your guest list. Here are how some of our party pals go about planning their guest list.

"Be specific and realistic when planning your party."

Molly Sims

"Overinviting makes for a good party. Controlled chaos is my goal."   Harry Morton

"According to my dearest friend, Lara Shriftman, one should always overinvite because there are always 'no-shows.'"

Michael Michele

three

YOU'RE INVITED

répondez, s'il vous plaît!

THE INVITATION PLAYS A LEADING ROLE IN EVERY EVENT

It's more than just a piece of paper; the invite is the host's opportunity to set the tone of the party and arm guests with all of the necessary information, from date to dress code.

One surefire way to ensure a seamless soiree is to explain to everyone exactly what you want. If you forget the address, date, or time, then your guests won't show up or, even worse, you'll spend the day of the party fielding a thousand questions about your event.

Our advice is simple: outline every single detail in the clearest terms on the invite. Not only does this rev up the guests' interest in attending, but also will make your job easier. Now you won't spend your precious planning time fielding pre-party inquisitions.

Before ordering your invitations be sure that you know the following details:

- The event date and time

- The address where it is taking place

- The correct spelling of any hosts' names and the locations

- The number of invitations you will need. Always order at least twenty-five extra per every fifty guests invited to account for mistakes or allow for additional invites. And double that of envelopes.

INVITATION 101

There are essential details that every invitation must include: Who (the hosts with the mostes'), What (why we're partying down), When (date, time), Where (location), and How (attire, though this subject is optional), and RSVP (that's the polite way of saying respond with a yes or no—or else!).

Sample invitations created for
Harrison & Shriftman

Photo credit: Myriam Santos

anatomy of an invitation

who The person(s) hosting the party

what Explain the purpose of the party. Be specific about the occasion and/or the person being honored so guests know what to expect. Instruct whether they should arrive armed with a gift, prepared dish, or just their smiling selves.

For example: (insert host(s) name here) invite you to a (type of event, reception, cocktail party, dinner, clambake, etc.) honoring (insert name of guest of honor here).

Or,

(insert host(s) name here) invite you to cocktails for (insert name of guest of honor here) birthday.

date The date of the event. We suggest including the day of the week to avoid any possible confusion.

The way the date is written generally depends on the type and degree of formality of the event. An informal invitation can read: Wednesday, August 1, 2008. A more formal approach spells out the date: Wednesday, the first of August, 2008.

time The time the event will begin and, when necessary, an end time. We only like to give end times when the event is only for a short span of time, say two hours, for example from 9 to 11 p.m.

In general, be as specific as possible about timing. The more explicit you are, the less likely you'll be spending the night coping with blunders. For example, avoid having to deal with dawdlers and write, "Come for cocktails at 7 p.m." or "Dinner will be served at 8 p.m." That way guests can plan accordingly.

The invitation is your line of communication, so choose your copy carefully. For example, for a seated dinner, let your guests know that fashionably late won't fly. Don't be afraid to use a pointed adjective like 9 o'clock "sharp" or 9 p.m. "on the dot," especially if you are working within a strict time frame (e.g., you only have your venue for two hours). Personally, Lara likes to spell it out literally, saying "8 o'clock in the evening."

location Explain where the event will take place. Include the name of the venue when applicable and the street address. So if you are hosting an in-suite soiree at a hotel, state the name of the hotel, and the specific room or area where the party will take place, and the street address.

attire Specify the dress code. Think "black tie" or "cocktail casual." This item is optional, but we strongly encourage you to include a note about suggested attire.

Specifying the preferred dress will save you and your guests time and grief. Guests appreciate guidance, so instead of saying business casual, consider a specific directive like "no denim" or "jackets required." Trust us, you don't want to spend your precious party prep-time fielding fashion inquiries from panicked couture-conscious attendees!

rsvp Indicate how you would like people to respond. If you opt for "regrets only" be sure to provide a contact number or e-mail. We prefer to make a phone call instead of e-mailing as it makes it more personal. If you must e-mail, do it only as a reminder and always, always bcc (blind carbon copy) so that you don't give out everyone's personal e-mails.

final step Proofread! Read your invitation forward and backward looking for any errors. Double-check dates, times, and spelling.

take note Depending on the space on your invitation, include other pertinent information including instructions for valet, gifts, or any invite details such as "this invite is nontransferable" or "this invite is extended to you and a guest." It's also appropriate to include "No gifts, please."

chic tip Every host should be adept at extending last-minute invites. Cancellations will always happen and you may have a seat that you must fill. Be preemptive and have a few substitutes in mind.

WHEN TO SEND

Nearly as important as the invitation is when you send it out. Timing can be tricky; send an invitation too late and guests may have other plans; send too early and the invitation might be misplaced, lost, or—dare we say—guests could forget. Yes, even though it's the only thing on your mind, it just might slip theirs.

We suggest that you extend the invitation at least two weeks before the date of the party, but no more than three weeks in advance. If guests will have to travel to attend, invitations must go out at least one month in advance, ideally sixty days, especially if you aren't footing the travel tab.

Remember to factor in mail time. Allow an extra couple of days for comrades on the other coast.

Budget Savers

Trying to save a few bucks on your invites? Here's a few points to consider.

- White or cream-colored paper usually costs less than decorative sheets.

- Heavier stock is the most expensive and may require more postage.

- Embellishments cost! While customizing with ribbons, overlays, colored inks, and letterpress looks great, it adds to the overall price. Go simple.

chic tip

If you're planning a party during the height of the holiday season or for any period when parties are common (like awards season in Los Angeles), send out your invitations four weeks in advance to ensure that your guests haven't already filled their party roster. And always follow up your invitation with a call to confirm attendance, as it's a polite way to remind people of your event during a busy time.

HOW TO SEND

We are still big proponents of sending out a "real" invitation. In fact, we suggest employing something like Evite only as a last resort or as a reminder. But Lara prefers to make phone calls as opposed to using e-mails or Evite. It's much more personal and makes the guests aware of how much you want them there.

Additionally, a tangible invitation makes the party seem more real and people tend to be more compelled to respond. Plus, most hard-working people are inundated with e-mails every day; receiving something material will get their attention. Once again, we have to bring up the effectiveness of a personal phone call—it's a guaranteed attention-getter!

Sure, there are times when an e-mail invitation is the way to go, like in the case of an impromptu party or when you're looking to save dinero, but again, picking up the phone and extending a warm, personal invite is just as effective.

By the same token, we suggest following up with a phone call one week after the invites go out and again twenty-four hours before the event to confirm attendance. The invite could get lost in the e-mail, someone's address may have changed, they may have been out of town, it's buried under a pile of unopened bills, the secretary misplaced it, you just never know! Likewise, be sure to follow up with the guests that you haven't heard from so you can have an accurate head count.

When you're calling people or if you are having someone else make the phone calls, make the job easier by writing out a script—yes, we're so Hollywood! But an outline ensures that every last detail is covered.

"Hi, I'm calling from Owen Wilson's office (Who). We'd love to invite you to a birthday party for Luke (Why), Friday, September 1, 2007, at 8 o'clock in the evening (When) at Il Sole, which is located at 8741 Sunset Boulevard (Where). It's a small, intimate dinner party and no gift is necessary (How). Please let me know if you can attend. Here is my number: (123) 456-7890. Please let me know by August 25th." (RSVP)

take note

If you do send via e-mail, always be sure to bcc (blind carbon copy) so that you don't send out everyone's personal e-mails; people hate that! If you don't bcc, then everyone knows who is coming to the party and nothing is left to the imagination! Someone could decide not to go to the party because they see who is invited. Sure, it works the other way as well—but we've found that in most cases it's the former that prevails.

THE MYSTERY MAN:
HOW DO YOU INVITE SOMEONE
YOU DON'T KNOW?

It's impossible to know every single person. Even the best of us, meaning those that work in the event industry where knowing anyone and everyone is a requirement of the job, don't know everyone. There's always someone new to the scene, someone who's making waves or just that guy or girl who has caught your eye. Generally, people like to go to parties that are filled with people they know, old friends, colleagues, a crowd of recognizable faces. But they also like to meet new people; after all, that's one of the reasons for throwing a party! Plus, it's fun for the host to have new faces at the party; spicing up the mix with old and new keeps your parties at the top of everyone's go-to list. Here's how to bring a new face to the party.

1. Come up with a targeted list of people you want to invite. Then think about who you know who knows those on the list and ask them to extend an invitation.

2. If your list is less specific, ask people who know interesting people for a list of prospects. Let them know who is coming so far and ask for recommendations of people they know who might fit in well with the group. This is a great approach when you're having a party and need more single guys or girls: turn to your solo pals for tips.

3. If there is a specific person you want to invite, go directly to them. Call them up and say, "Look, I'm having a party. I know we don't know each other but I would really love it if you would attend. I'd love to get to know you better." Done and done! If you don't feel comfortable placing a personal phone call, send a note asking the same thing. But be realistic, don't expect to send Brad Pitt a note and expect him to show up! This is not a method for stalking!

4. Look for a hook. Perhaps you are planning a benefit and you know a particular person is involved with or is really interested in the cause; that's the perfect introduction.

5. Think big! A large guest list or easy-breezy cocktail party is the type of event to invite a newbie to. Don't invite a relative stranger to a small intimate gathering like a dinner party or a personal event like a wedding or baby or bridal shower. That's just plain creepy!

ADDRESS 101

In the past, it was simple: man and woman marry, woman takes man's last name. Not anymore! Many women opt to keep their maiden name or hyphenate. These developments, not to mention other trends in unconventional living situations à la cohabitation, make addressing an envelope very complex and often mind-boggling.

ENVELOPE ETIQUETTE

Don't neglect your envelope! It's the first thing guests see, even before they see the perfectly penned invite.

Envelope protocol depends on the type of event you are throwing. If you are sending a formal invitation (like a wedding) use both inner and outer envelopes. Address the outer envelope to the primary invitee(s) and only people who live at the address to which you are sending the invitation. If your invitation is for the invitee and a guest, address the inner envelope to both the primary invitee "and guest."

When sending an informal invitation, there is no need for layers of envelopes. If it is an "and guest" occasion, throwing a "plus one" on the invitation will do the trick. Guests, pay attention! If the envelope contains your name only, that means you're going solo.

chic tip   Couple code: if a couple (gay or straight) lives together, then they are invited together. The same goes for a couple who are engaged but don't live together. You can't invite one without the other!

take note   Traditionally a man's name comes before the woman's on the envelope, but nowadays, it doesn't really matter. Do what feels right to you.

Married Couple | Same last names

Mr. and Mrs. Milo Peterson

Married Couple | Different last names
(e.g., woman uses her maiden name)

Mr. Milo Peterson and Ms. Lulu Flynn (vice versa okay)

Unmarried, but live together

Mr. Milo Peterson

Ms. Lulu Flynn

TRICKY TITLES

On a casual invite, you may opt to use first names only (Milo and Lulu). Make sure you use proper designations—believe us, people get offended if you don't. Save Miss for girls under the age of eighteen. While all women love to feel young, there is something about Miss that feels a bit juvenile. On the other hand, Ms. is always safe. If you are not sure if a woman prefers to be called Mrs., don't risk offending her and just default to Ms.

problem Both recipients are doctors (either Ph.D. or medical) and have the same last name.

s o l u t i o n   Drs. Milo and Lulu Peterson, or Dr. Milo Peterson and Dr. Lulu Peterson (vice versa is okay)

p r o b l e m   Both recipients are doctors (either Ph.D. or medical) and the woman uses her maiden name.

s o l u t i o n   Dr. Milo Peterson and Dr. Lulu Flynn (vice versa is okay)

p r o b l e m   Inviting a guest

s o l u t i o n   Lulu Flynn and Guest

p r o b l e m   Children are not invited.

s o l u t i o n   Address the invite to Mr. and Mrs. Stan Stanley instead of writing the Stanley Family. You may also carve out some space on the invite pointing out that kids are not welcome by saying something along the lines of: A nursery and babysitter will be provided for children.

PROFESSIONAL PROTOCOL

When sending an invitation for a personal party to someone's place of work, you should observe certain parameters. In this case, professional designations take the place of traditional titles. When sending an invite to a place of business be sure to write the company name on the second line, above the address.

Thus, when sending your annual Christmas invitation to your beloved CPA, lose the Ms. or Mr. Instead, use Lulu Flynn, CPA. If you are inviting the legal clan use either Lulu Flynn, Esq., or Ms. Lulu Flynn, Attorney at Law, on two lines.

THE LOOK

The design of an invitation should reflect the character of the event; after all, it's the first impression! Everything about the design of the invitation, down to the words you choose, sets the tone for the party in your guests' minds.

Include as much information as possible without interrupting the aesthetic or tone of the invitation. Catchy text is always welcome and even encouraged, but not at the expense of clarity. For example, including dress suggestions like "casual" or "beach formal" is fantastic creative copy, but it is also pretty vague. Does beach formal mean you should wear a gold-flocked bikini, or white linen?

One of the biggest problems is contending with unannounced guests. Be preemptive and do your part to make sure that your invitation makes it perfectly clear whether or not such additions are allowed. For larger events consider adding text like "this invitation nontransferable." If an invitation is meant for the invitee and a guest, make that clear.

THE WRITE STUFF

Finding the perfect words is always a challenge. Choosing the right language is even more difficult when faced with any number of sticky scenarios such as when you host a party at a restaurant but you don't plan on footing the bill. How do you let your guests know they are responsible for their own meal without sounding cheap? Our chart helps you find the perfect wordplay to handle such party conundrums.

problem **"No gifts!"**

solution "In lieu of gifts, please donate to (insert name of guest of honor's favorite charity). Or, don't mince words and just say it: "No gifts, please!"

problem **Cash bar**

solution **Bring your bucks!** Cocktails will be served at a cash bar. (Lara and Elizabeth find this incredibly tacky. If you're going to throw a party, either have the moolah to do it or enlist hosts. The only time a cash bar is acceptable is when the event is for charity.)

problem **BYOB**

solution Please bring your favorite beverage. (Guests, by the way, should be aware that in a BYOB situation, they should plan on leaving excess booze with the host. We think this should be reserved for college frat parties only!)

problem **Fixed menu with set price per guest**

solution "$35 per person all-inclusive." (You can even get more specific: "$35 includes appetizer, entrée, dessert, tax, and gratuity.")

problem **Guests of guests are not welcome.**

solution "This invite is nontransferable."

take note   We firmly believe that when you are throwing a party you should never ask or expect your guests to pay for anything. The host, and if there is one, the committee, should handle all expenses. If you can't afford to cover all the costs, then consider a different, less expensive alternative.

These are times when surprises are not welcome! So be crystal-spanking clear when inviting guests. Let them know if they are expected to pay for anything, although we firmly believe that if you have invited guests to a dinner, you should be paying.

TRICKY TEXT

There are many ways to convey information. For example, when telling guests what time the party begins you could write 7 P.M. or "seven o'clock in the evening." We prefer the latter, but either is okay.

How you choose to lay out your invitation depends on the type of event. Formal events call for formal language. For example, the symbol "+1" or the phrase "plus one" should never appear on any type of formal invite. Rather, use the conventional term "and guest."

ABBREVIATION ABANDON

If space permits, we always suggest spelling words out, both on the invitation and the envelope. For example, if you have room, use "Street" or "Boulevard" instead of "St." or "Blvd." And, yes, we like directions to be spelled out. Whether you abbreviate or not, be consistent. If you settle on "St.," then employ the shortened versions of street addresses throughout, such as "Apt." or "Bldg." You get the idea!

HOW TO SAY NO TO AN INVITE

Just say no! Sure, that sounds easy enough, but often you hear yourself saying yes because you are caught off guard by the invite or can't think of a reason why you can't come to a particular event. Keep in mind that you don't have to explain why you are not available; attending a party is a choice, not a requirement! Be firm, thank the host for the invitation, and say no. But sometimes, no just isn't enough. Here's an arsenal of reasons why not.

"You have a previous engagement."   Dani Janssen

"I say I am on location."   Hugh Jackman

"Graciously decline in a timely manner."   Michael Michele

"Saying no to an invitation is easy. I just say no. Or I say I have something else to do on that evening, which is usually the case for me!"   Serena Williams

HOW DO YOU CONFIRM ATTENDANCE?

While we recommend following up on RSVPs with a personal phone call, other hosts have their own methods. We asked some of the best hosts we know how they follow up with guests.

"I start early with a personal telephone call. If they accept, then I call their assistant and ask them to put the date in their book. If they're not sure for some reason, then I ask them to call me one week before the party date to verify. At that time the list will be complete. After that I'm too busy cooking to answer the phone. This way I have a week to invite others to fill in the original number of guests."   Dani Janssen

"I make personal calls and I will also send an e-mail."
                                                        Michael Michele

"Send a reminder e-mail a few days before. Confirmation is necessary."   Molly Sims

"I call them personally if they haven't RSVPd."   Vanna White

HOW FAR IN ADVANCE SHOULD YOU SEND THE INVITES OUT?

Knowing when to send an invitation is key; often it depends on the type of party you are throwing. For Harrison & Shriftman events we usually get invites in the mail two weeks in advance.

"I've received a save the date for a Bat Mitzvah almost one year in advance. Bat Mitzvah invites usually go out about two months prior to the party. If you're having a regular birthday or holiday party, you're okay with just a month. If it's just going to be a few people, two weeks is fine. I usually don't make follow-up calls, but for my Halloween party, Lisa will call and confirm any unresponded to RSVPs."   Sophia Schrager

four

MIND YOUR P'S & Q'S

an fyi for all you pyts

GOOD BEHAVIOR IS EVERYTHING Didn't your mama teach you anything? This chapter will have you flowing with good graces in just one reading. We will show you how to put the pen to paper and write a wonderful thank-you note (yes, they are required!), make introductions, and cover the ground on conversation winners—and losers! Here are the common customs that you should live and party by, no matter which side of the soiree you are on.

THREE OCCASIONS TO BE THANKFUL

Be thankful upon receipt of a gift, and that includes presents by mail and messenger—even a floral delivery. It's especially important in the case of a mailed gift, as the sender wants to know it arrived, so pull out the stationery and send a note, stat!

Be thankful after attending a party at someone's home. Don't get us wrong, we suggest guests write a post-party thank-you note to their hosts—period. However, it is especially important to be obliged when someone has opened their home to you. And even more so if you, dare we say, made any sort of gaffe, no matter how small, because your thankfulness will go a long way, baby!

Be thankful when someone does something incredibly thoughtful, whether it's as simple as taking you to lunch on a particularly rough day, or being a friend who is always there.

THE WRITE STUFF

1. **SHORT 'N' SWEET** This is the universal rule of note writing, make it meaningful but succinct. A note is not a novel!

2. **BE HANDS ON** In general, we prefer a handwritten note, as it's more personal and thoughtful. But if your handwriting resembles scribbles on a doctor's pad, get thee to a computer and get creative with fonts. This doesn't mean it's acceptable to fire off an e-mail. Hitting send is so, yawn, apathetic.

3. **TECHNOLOGICALLY ACCEPTABLE** There are a few instances where we can (sort of) rationalize an electronic expression of gratitude. An e-mail is acceptable for a gift that was ordered online; after all, it's already computer generated! An e-mail will also suffice for larger, less personal events where you may not have interacted with the host.

4. **SPELL CHECK** To err may be human, but a misspelled note is embarrassing! Who can forget the fateful *Sex and the City* episode when Big's new wife sends Carrie a note saying "I'm so sorry I couldn't be their." Gasp! Thoroughly check your notes for spelling (especially the spelling of the name of the person you are addressing) and grammar. A blatant error is careless and distracting. There's nothing worse than addressing Lara as Laura!

5. **PERMANENT MARKER** It's not grade school, so don't write in pencil. Buy a beautiful colored pen and make it your signature.

For example, Lara uses personalized white cardstock and with an orange pen she crosses out her name at the top with a flourish and writes a quick, clever note.

take note

A handwritten thank-you note is one of the most powerful forms of communication; and the fact that they are becoming increasingly rare makes them even more valuable. Writing a proper thank-you note is one of the most important elements of being a good guest, not to mention a powerful tool that will help protect your slot at the top of everyone's list. And, as a host, part of receiving a gift gracefully is following through with a proper acknowledgment.

chic tip

Flowers should always have a personal touch. Take the time to drop off a handwritten note at the florist ahead of time. Try to find out if they have a favorite flower or florist. For example, Lara adores orchids and floating gardenias, so that's the way to her heart! Remember, arriving with flowers at a party isn't the best move, since it requires the host or honoree to stop what they are doing and find a suitable vase or display.

ANATOMY OF A THANK-YOU NOTE

Every note should be customized and tailored to the recipient but the basic structure is essentially the same: a greeting, note of appreciation, and a mention of how the item or event will be useful and/or enjoyed. Close with the proposition of a future meeting. This construction is relatively fail-safe, although the last component can be omitted when necessary.

the greeting

Just as it sounds—"Dear Lucas" or "My Darling (or Dearest) Ava."

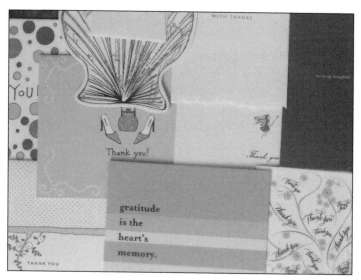

Assortment of thank-you cards

the appreciation

This is a requisite of any thank-you note. It's your moment to express gratitude for a great party, sentiment, favor, gift, or whatever. Be specific because you do not want your message to seem like a generic form letter: "Thank you for the stunning (a token adjective never hurts) Peter Som sweater."

the mention

A specific appreciation sets you up perfectly for the "mention," which explains how the sentiment, favor, or gift was or will be useful, fun, glorious, incredible, or whatever adjective best describes your happiness. If you are thanking your host after a dinner party, be sure to say how fabulous the night was and how much you enjoyed yourself.

the proposition

Whenever appropriate, end a note by suggesting a future meeting. If this is too strong, opt for something vague. We find "Hope to see you soon" works well. If even that is a stretch, then go for the simple, but straightforward "Thank you again" before signing off.

Thank-You Template

Hate the thank-you note? We'll make your job a bit easier by laying it out, word for word. All you have to do is fill in the blanks!

Dear/Darling/Dearest/Hello!

_____

(recipient's name),

Thank you for the lovely/amazing/adorable/handsome/stylish/ exquisite/funky

_____

(enter type of gift).

I look forward to using/wearing/displaying/enjoying/

_____

(enter gift again) **for years to come/at the holidays/this summer/every day.**

Can't wait to see/meet/talk/catch up/visit/ you at

_____

(location or time) **at the party/wedding/during the holidays/after the party/at the water cooler/at dinner next week.**

Sincerely/Warmly/Fondly/Love/Cheers/ Best!

_____

(sign your name)

SIGNED, SEALED, AND DELIVERED

Almost as important as crafting the perfect note is sending it in a timely matter. Bottom line, send notes promptly! Aim to get it in the mail within one week of the event, favor, or gift. Anything after two weeks and the impact is diluted. That being said, we firmly believe it's never too late. An exceedingly delayed note is not an excuse to skip the process! Sit down and write a more general note, and mention that you feel terrible for not writing earlier to thank them for their astounding thoughtfulness.

PAPER POWER

Presentation is everything. Clichéd? Yes. True? Undeniably. While we are admitted paper snobs, there are some guidelines to consider when choosing your canvas; after all, choice of stationery says a lot about a person. We are not implying that you should stock the finest stationery available, but we do suggest having a small reserve of nice cards for special occasions. Lara's favorite local LA spot is the Paper Source, an amazing boutique that has reams in all shapes, sizes, and types—casual, formal, elegant, whimsical, and more.

chic tip

Splurge on a set of personalized cards and keep them in your office. They will add that extra personal touch and make it easier on you to get the note-writing job done. Lara always puts a pen-drawn slash through her typewritten name on every card she sends out. Recipients always ask why she does that and it's simply to add a personal touch to every note.

Samples of personal stationery

Photo credit: Myriam Santos

take note   If you opt for a commercial greeting card, don't ever simply sign and send. Please, no matter how short the sentiment, take the time to add a personal note in order to inject a bit of you into the card.

ENVELOPE ETIQUETTE

Even before the recipient lays eyes on your perfect prose (on fabulous card stock, of course), they will see the envelope. We prefer our envelopes, like our notes, to be handwritten. That being said, legible is the foremost requirement. If you have less than satisfactory penmanship, pick a beautiful typewritten font and go with it.

take note   Many execs, doctors, and lawyers have an assistant open their mail, so when sending a note to someone's place of work, write "personal" or "via messenger" in the lower right or left corner of the envelope. This way, the note stays personal and the recipient can enjoy from start to finish.

DIALOGUE DECORUM

Lively conversation is a central component of any fabulous party. But for some, the thought of making small talk and idle chatter is daunting, dreadful, and painful. No matter if you are the party-thrower or the partygoer, polished conversation skills are a must. You need to know what should and shouldn't be said, and how to bail yourself out of any banter blunder. There are certain things that will keep you afloat even amid the most taxing tête-à-tête.

- A key thing to remember is that party conversation should be light and generally upbeat. One overarching directive to keep in mind is don't be controversial, and unless you know someone really well, avoid divisive issues like politics and religion.

- Listen a lot and intently. The best way to avoid blunders is to listen more than you speak. Likewise, ask a lot of questions, specifically ones that don't loop the conversation back to you.

- At all costs, avoid yes or no questions; they will get you nowhere! Instead pose open-ended questions, like "What movies have you seen lately?" Such queries help maintain momentum and keep the conversation flowing.

- Never assume anything in casual conversation. Assumption usually segues to a verbal blunder.

Is the silent pause making the night move slower than molasses? Get the party moving by putting Table Topics into action. This fun, lively collection of questions breaks the ice and gets everyone talking— even polar opposites. We especially love the cards at dinner parties when bringing a group of people together who might be meeting for the first time. Some of our favorite questions: If you could have dinner anywhere in the world, which restaurant would you choose?

Which pet is your favorite? If you could spend one week at any hotel in the world, where would you go?

When people ask any questions that make you uncomfortable, take the power back with this sure-fire response: "That's very personal, why do you ask?" The key is to smile and have a very open and pleasant expression. Don't be confrontational; make it a friendly interlude while at the same time putting the discomfort back on the person who asked the invasive question!

Crimes of Conversation

DON'T	DO
Interrupt	Make eye contact
Brag	Listen
Ask how old someone is	Ask open-ended questions
Dominate the conversation	Ask about their interests
Talk nonstop about yourself	Be engaging
Look around the room while in a conversation	
Ask invasive questions about someone's age, whether they are pregnant, and so on, or you might end up red faced	

VERBAL BLUNDERS

problem **Saying exactly what you're thinking.** Yep, everyone's done it. You find yourself rambling on about how much you can't stand the outfit Paris Hilton is wearing tonight, only to discover you just said that to the designer. Can we say awkward?

solution **Don't take yourself or the situation so seriously.** Try making a lighthearted joke or soften the blow by saying something along the lines of "What do I know about fashion?" If you stuck your foot in your mouth by saying something controversial or brought up a nonparty subject like religion or politics, make a comment about how you should know better than to bring up such a controversial subject! "My mother taught me better than this!" and then change the subject. Quickly. Don't backtrack because you'll just come across as insincere.

problem **Gossip gets you in trouble.** You've just met the man of your dreams and while you're gabbing gloriously you decide to tell him the hilarious story you heard recently about a high-profile CEO who's been cheating on his wife with his nanny. So Jude Law, right? Yikes. Turns out the CEO is Mr. Right's father.

solution **Explaining yourself will only make the situation worse.** The best thing to do is sincerely apologize and mean it. Then make note of this situation for future reference and leave the gossipy tales for your bestest friend.

p r o b l e m **Congratulations!** You squeal upon noticing Lauren's particularly plump tummy. But instead of hearing all the details of the sonogram and baby's room, you see Lauren's face turn bright red as she announces she's *not* preggers.

s o l u t i o n **Ouch. Grovel, grovel, and then grovel some more.** Mistaking plumpness for pregnancy is one of the most uncomfortable moments. Let Lauren know how stupid you feel, apologize, and get out of her sight—fast! To smooth over the sour water, consider writing a heartfelt note after the fact to apologize again.

p r o b l e m **Carol has been planning a surprise party for her boyfriend, Matt, for the past month.** You're looking forward to the big night so much that when you see Matt you blurt out, "Are you ready for the big party?" Surprise no more.

s o l u t i o n **You can't take it back now.** The cat is out of the bag so you'd better buy one fabulous gift. Admit to the host your mistake and send her flowers to apologize for your gabby gaffe. And in the future? If you can't keep a secret, avoid the guest of honor in the days leading up to the big event. That way you won't have to worry about spoiling the surprise.

DIFFUSING DISASTERS

One of the most important things in maneuvering your way through a conversation is to know how to salvage a dialogue gone badly. Whether a chat has slid into dangerous territory, or the dreaded awkward pause has reared its ugly head, both a good host and guest must know how to handle the situation with ease.

problem **The conversation takes an uncomfortable turn.**
You're busy dishing with Sally, a once-in-a-while party pal, and Kelly, your b-f-f. Out-of-the-loop Sally inquires about the absence of Kelly's live-in boyfriend of ten years. You know full well that the couple just had a huge fight and Kelly has since moved out. A night of tears and drama looms!

solution **Find neutral ground as quickly and effortlessly as possible.** Steer Sally in another direction by saying something along the lines of "Maybe we should talk about that another time." And then quickly introduce Kelly to someone new in order to redirect her attention (for the moment, anyway).

problem **Age restrictions.** No, he *didn't!* You were just introduced to Bob, who after making small talk asked your age.

solution **Keep your lips sealed.** When faced with a prying question such as this do not feel like you have to answer. The best response is a gentle chiding with a smile: "You never ask a woman (or man!) her age!" It is also perfectly acceptable to respond with an even-keeled answer like "I'd rather not say." Being straight up, versus skirting the issue or responding with a vague retort, is another way to escape deeper probing. If perfectly frank isn't your style, turn the question around and inquire, "Why do you ask?" At the very least, this tactic will buy you some time to plot a reply. Or play coy and respond with "I'm a twenty (thirty, forty, and so on) something."

p r o b l e m   **The rambler.** You're having a great time when you get cornered by Tom, a notorious rambler who proceeds to recount, in excruciating detail, his recent surgery. You've been listening to his list of dietary restrictions for twenty minutes. How do you escape without being offensive?

s o l u t i o n   **There are a couple of options.** You can excuse yourself politely to use the restroom or refresh your drink, grin and bear it, or jump in and lead the errant chatterbox onto a different conversation track. Help him or her get to the point by asking targeted questions. In this sleep-inducing situation ambiguous questions (the category under which most "courtesy questions" fall) will only hurt your cause. If posing a precise question doesn't work, excuse yourself to the restroom or to the bar. Chances are, in your absence, the talker will have found a new victim!

p r o b l e m   **A stand-up comedy routine gone bad, really bad.** Mr. Comedy Man? Not so amusing. Yes, it happens. You find yourself achingly uncomfortable when a party-goer tells a joke or hilarious story that far from tickles anyone's funny bone.

solution **Laughter really is the best**—and the only—medicine in this case. Don't overdo it with a belly-busting guffaw—a polite giggle will suffice.

problem **The phone number exchange.** Sam just met the woman of his dreams, now he wants to get her seven digits. What's the best move to make?

solution **Be tactful, be polite.** If you don't feel like being upfront with the man or woman of your dreams, ask the host to assist in the number game. Keep in mind that a host (or anyone, for that matter) should never, ever hand out personal information such as a phone number or e-mail address without the individual's permission. If someone approaches you in search of a number, you can either ask the person they are trying to reach if they are okay with sharing their information or give out a public number, maybe their workplace or assistant. Another method is to offer to pass along the requestor's information.

Or you just met the woman of your dreams, great smile, gorgeous eyes, and a kickin' body with the personality to match. Problem is, she's on the arm of another man. Leave it to Stephen Dorff to find the perfect way to get a taken woman's seven digits. He recommends keeping it simple by asking, "How can I find you if I need to send you a gift or something?" What girl doesn't love that!

problem **Single Sally has finally fallen in love.** In fact, she's been raving about George since the day she met him, but the name is about the only thing her guy has in common with that other delectable dish, George Clooney. In other words, he's a dog with a raunchy personality to match. Now she's cornered you and asking what you think of him: "Isn't he cute?"

solution **Honesty is not always the best policy,** especially in this case. So forget what you really think of his looks and say something along the lines of "Well, he's not my type, but I'm so glad you're happy with him." Or point out something that you do find attractive about him, perhaps his sense of humor or that chic Armani suit he's wearing.

problem **You haven't seen your pal Nicole in ages.** And from the looks of her, she's definitely had some work done on her nose, eyes . . . and is her forehead suffering from a severe case of Botox? Yes, in this modern time where plastic surgery is a way of life, you're bound to encounter a friend who's had some tweaks. Question is, do you ask?

solution **Don't say anything until she does.** You can invite conversation by complimenting her on how great she looks or ask if she's been doing anything different, did she lose weight, get a new facialist? Don't push. If she wants to talk about it, she will! If it's an old friend, you can attack the obvious by making light of the new look: "We've been friends for fifteen years and I know that's not your nose!"

chic tip

When you find yourself at a party with a group of semi-strangers, the awkward pause in conversation is nearly inevitable. Remember, it is safe to assume that everyone at the party knows the host. When all else fails, default to this common denominator and ask, "How do you know Elizabeth?" Or "Lara really outdid herself tonight! Did you taste those bacon-wrapped dates?"

take note

Bilingual partiers, if you know the common language, speak it. A perfectly innocent conversation, even in one of the romance languages, scares nonfluent folks to the other side of the room. And no matter what language you speak, the most important directive is to keep your conversation topics light, fun, and entertaining. Leave the heavy religious, political, and emotionally charged subject matter for a night at home with your best, best friends. Controversial topics can leave a bad taste in a guest's mouth—and send a soiree spiraling downward in no time.

PLEASED TO MEET YOU

the host

- Making introductions is undeniably an important role of a host. Encouraging guests to mingle is your responsibility, especially at the outset. We always suggest giving "introducees" seeds of conversation before leaving them alone to fend for themselves. Find a slice of common ground to get the conversation flowing. "Lisa, this is Lew. He is the CFO of Coach and I know you're a huge fan of their handbags!" Move on while Lisa grills Lew on their latest line.

- When introducing a man and woman, address the woman first. Likewise, when introducing people of different ages, speak to the elder first.

- Use first and last names. If you do not know someone's last name, keep it consistent and introduce the other party using their first name only as well.

the guest

Introductions may be the host's responsibility, but the guests aren't allowed to just stand there and watch the host work. There are parameters for the flip side of an introduction.

- Use the name that was said when the introduction was made. In other words, if your host introduces you to her hunky cousin Matthew, as far as you're concerned he is Matthew, not Matt or any other variation. Never assume it's your right to arbitrarily employ a nickname!

- This is . . . uh . . . If it becomes obvious your host has drawn a sudden blank when it comes time to say your name, don't take offense, it happens! Come to their rescue by extending your hand and introducing yourself.

"You look mah-velous, my darling." Now it's your turn to say thank you. Don't respond by listing everything that went wrong with your makeup, hair, outfit, and emotional state. While self-deprecation can be effective in select instances, this is not one. Be modest, say thank you, and most of all, do not protest or disagree—because that type of response will come across as insecurity and people may think you are searching for more compliments. Smile, you do look pretty!

TOP FIVE CONVERSATION STARTERS

The introduction has been made and now you're wondering where to go next. Break the ice with one of these tried and true lines.

1. "I've heard a lot about you!"

2. Compliment someone's shoes, bag, outfit, hair, eyes . . . anything!

3. Ask how they know the host or guest of honor.

4. Skip the politics and opt for talking about the latest film, book, TV show, or musical artist.

5. You can never go wrong with the weather or travel! "Been on any vacations lately?" is sure to spark a good story.

Southern Comfort

Take a cue from Bruce Taylor, a perfectly fine southern gentleman (and one of Lara's favorites) who lives a gracious, well-mannered life in Jacksonville, Florida.

- Always respect your elders.

- Stand when a lady enters or leaves the room.

- Never discuss health, wealth, or religion.

- No matter a person's station in life, everyone is deserving of respect.

- Treat another man's dog as you would treat your children.

- If faced with an argument, remember: even a thin slice of ham has two sides.

- Always give thanks for your meal.

- If God meant us to have cell phones at the dinner table, they would be in the recipe!

- There is no substitute for a handwritten letter.

 take note   A host should make a point to introduce each person to three people. Follow this rule of introductions and your guests will be mixing and mingling like pros.

NOW, THIS IS FUNNY

Telling a good joke is a talent. Not everyone is adept at delivering a pitch-perfect funny bone tickler. In fact, ruining a joke is the easiest thing to do—all it takes is a botched intro, a forgotten line, or bad timing. The good news is that you don't have to be Jerry Seinfeld to get a laugh out of the crowd. It just takes a bit of practice—yes, it's time to get in front of the mirror! Believe us, it works.

MEMORIZE The key is to prepare ahead of time. Know the joke inside and out, rehearse it until you know it by heart. Nothing kills a laugh faster than starting and restarting a joke.

THE SETUP This is the core of the joke. It contains all of the necessary information, establishes the setting, the players, and the situation. There should be enough clues to make the punch line satisfying.

THE PUNCH LINE This is the reveal so don't mess it up! It should be delivered with perfect comedic timing, a slight pause right before you deliver the final line so that everyone knows that this is the clincher. Cue raucous laughter.

A FEW REMINDERS Don't tell jokes that have questionable subject matter, specifically those with racial or religious undertones.

BEST DRESSED!

Designer Catherine Malandrino knows a thing or two about what to wear. Follow her tips and you'll be the best-dressed girl at the party.

catherine malandrino's top five dos

1. Dresses with beautiful heels—always!

2. Make a statement simple and chic.

3. Dress suggestive instead of revealing.

4. Playing with transparencies or cutouts is always more sensual.

5. Make it yours and unique—be daring with a special color or embroidery.

and the don'ts

1. Don't mix it with sneakers.

2. Avoid the easy jeans and top.

3. Don't show too much skin.

4. Don't play it too done; keeping it "effortless" is always more sensual.

the perfect oufit for a . . .

DINNER PARTY	A dress that flirts with the knee, with bare leg and heels
BEACH PARTY	Bare feet, a long dress to the floor suspended by straps. Bangles!
SUNDAY BRUNCH	A knit dress with ballerina flats
COCKTAIL PARTY	A colorful silk chiffon embroidered dress flirting with the knee, with high heel sandals

FIVE FASHION DOS AND DON'TS FROM DESIGNER PETER SOM

dos

1. Do wear those fabulous sky high (yet totally impractical) stilettos. This is the time to do it.

2. Do have fun with bold jewelry.

3. Do pack only what you need in your clutch—credit card, ID, phone, lipstick, cash.

4. Do remember a cover-up—it can be warm outside and freezing inside. Borrowing your date's jacket should be a last resort.

5. Do show some skin—but focus only on one area. Decolletage neckline? Don't go mini. Dress with a crazy side slit? Try something with sleeves. A little mystery is very sexy.

don'ts

1. Don't wear a wrap in the same fabric as your dress. You are not going to a prom (nor do you want to look like upholstery).

2. Don't carry around your day purse. Nothing ruins a chic dress like a big clunky leather bag with everything but the kitchen sink in it.

3. Don't overdo the makeup—there's a fine line between an evening look and a drag queen look. A fresh face will always be chic.

4. Don't just wear black. We love our LBDs (little black dresses) but try a fun color and stand out of the crowd.

5. Don't forget the proper "support" if you're wearing something low cut, slightly sheer, or very tight. Keep your girls in place!

WHAT'S THE BEST PIECE OF ETIQUETTE ADVICE YOU'VE HEARD?

Some of the best pieces of advice are those that have been passed down through the generations or are derived from a personal experience. Our history of throwing parties at Harrison & Shriftman has spawned a book, so just imagine what other frequent party-goers have learned. Here are a few of our favorite tips from friends.

- Always dress appropriately.

- It is okay to be fashionably late.

- Cancel even if last minute.

- Don't make an ass out of yourself.

- Don't be too loud.

- Treat the venue as if it were your own.

- Extinguish cigarette butts in appropriate places if you smoke.

"Relax and be yourself and if you can't be yourself and be relaxed, be someone who is. Pretend you're someone fabulous, like Diane Von Furstenberg; strike a pose and believe it. Also, don't move around too much. Find your place and let the party

come to you. And remember what your mother said—a smile is the perfect accessory."   Gigi Levangie Grazer,
author of *Maneater* and *The Starter Wife*

"Your ability to mingle and converse is always helpful. Educate yourself not only about your own interests, but current and past world events. Intellect draws listeners."   Michael Michele

"My advice to the hosts: always have plenty of food on hand for surprise guests. Be laid back, life is stressful enough without having to lose sleep over throwing a dinner party."

David Arquette

five

GUESTLY MANNERS

good graces to get you on the a-list

HAPPY TO LET SOMEONE ELSE DO THE PLANNING WHILE YOU DO THE PARTYING? Not so fast, my social butterfly. There are a set of guiding principles for the party guest. As the invitee, you have an equally important role in ensuring the success of even the most sublime party. In fact, while the host sets the tone for the party, the guests are the key to ensuring that the dynamic is carried on through to the last cocktail—or at least dessert. This chapter arms you with must-know information that will keep you on the top of everyone's list and deciphers the unspoken guest code of conduct.

RSVP

Your responsibility as a guest begins upon receiving an invitation (and yes, though we hate to say it and don't suggest you use them, Evites do count). Nearly every invitation sent out requests a response. It's a simple request, really, and taking the time to reply will definitely safeguard your spot on the A-list. When RSVP'ing do not ask who else is coming.

the rules of response

1. ALWAYS RSVP It is courteous to inform the host of your plans, whether you are able to attend or not. The answer no is just as important to your host as "yes" when planning the party. The only exception to this rule is if an invitation asks for "regrets only." Yes, we are all busy, but no one is too swamped to respond properly to an invitation.

2. TIME IS TICKING Let your host know as soon as you possibly can of your plans. Ideally, we suggest that you RSVP within two days of receiving an invitation. If a reply card is included (it's not hard, it's stamped and ready to go!), be certain to respond by the date noted. When you are invited with a guest, it's nice to offer the name of the person you will be bringing.

3. DECLINE GRACEFULLY If you will be out of town on the date of Betsey's Thirty-fifth Blowout, you must let her know that you will be otherwise occupied. It's the right thing to do! Since a host has to plan according to numbers, knowing who will not be there is just as important as knowing who will be there.

4. DON'T GIVE LONG AND DRAWN-OUT REASONS-CUM-EXCUSES FOR A NO REPLY Attending, or not attending, is your prerogative. Believe it or not, your host doesn't necessarily need (or care) to know about your pup's latest bout with kennel cough, or the details of your current family crisis. The Party CEO is merely trying to secure an accurate head count. Remember, honesty is the best policy. If the plain truth isn't acceptable (or too embarrassing for whatever unimaginable reason) you can never go wrong with the defense of a prior engagement.

5. FOLLOW INSTRUCTIONS When an invitation states a preferred method of reply, use it! Call the number provided, send the e-mail, or put the reply card in the mail. Otherwise, responding can be as simple as sending an e-mail to your host.

Something as basic as this will always suffice: "Thank you for the invitation. I will not be able to make it but would love to connect soon. I know the party will be amazing!"

The above takes nine seconds to type in an e-mail and send (that includes a couple of extra seconds for those of us who have a very close relationship with the backspace key).

6. COMMITMENT ISSUES? Get some therapy but first, contact the host and acknowledge your receipt of the invitation. Let them know that you will reconnect once you can confirm. Sure, it's only a party (and you have what, ten deadlines to meet at the moment?), but remember that your host has put time (and cash) into planning, and needs to execute accordingly—especially in cases where numbers are important. And, face it, no host wants to tap into their B-list unnecessarily!

7. SAYING NOTHING IS NOT AN OPTION Nonresponsiveness is never acceptable and not okay by any standards. Quite frankly, silence is unacceptable in our current era of constant communication, cell phones, BlackBerry . . . come on, you can find a spare moment! Very few excuses are even conceivable in the age of nearly boundless access to some form of correspondence. Besides, a punctual RSVP is a good way to ensure a repeat invitation.

8. YES MEANS YES! RSVP'ing is only step one. Now you must also honor the commitment. Being a no-show is the quickest way to get dropped from any guest list. If you must cancel on

account of a bona fide emergency or conflict, call your host immediately so they can make any necessary adjustments. Not going at all is not an option. It's imperative that you call and alert your host even if it is at the last minute (and this is one seriously rude move, so you'd better have a rock solid excuse!). Calling is especially important for smaller events where your absence would be noticed (e.g., a seated dinner). If you are unable to connect with your host the day of the event, follow up the following day and apologize *profusely*.

9. THE OLD SWITCHEROO Changing a yes to a no, even in advance, should be avoided. If you have committed to attend, then go. Conversely, changing a no reply to a yes is okay, but only if it will not upset the host's plans. Do not assume that a positive reply exempts you from following up with your host. To your host, you are not just a body, you are also an additional place setting or one more bottle of Grey Goose. You get the idea, so keep the lines of communication open.

Other Rules of Returns

Any call that is placed must be returned the same day. Any response after twenty-four hours is rude but you really do have up until two days. Apologize with a simple "Sorry." If you absolutely cannot get to their call, shoot off an e-mail that explains you are incredibly busy, traveling, or unable to call at that time and let them know when they can expect a call. The same etiquette applies to e-mail, so make it snappy!

PLUS-ONE PROTOCOL

If we had to apply a faux pas rating scale, coming to a party with an unannounced guest would certainly rank as guest etiquette violation number one. There is nothing tackier than showing up with an unexpected guest in tow. The tenet we live by is "guests of guests may not bring guests." It is important to remember that a guest list is formulaic. Your host has deliberately and carefully crafted a list of specific people to invite. If he or she wanted to mix things up by having you bring your crush from the office, they'd let you know.

The bottom line: unless an invitation specifically states "and guest," don't bring one. Don't even ask! Only the person listed on the invitation is to attend—period. This is especially important for formal events or seated dinners where the head count is specific. That being said, a larger event does not grant you license to search for a hot date. If you are absolutely desperate to bring your best bud or have an out-of-town guest, you must clear it with your host ahead of time.

SOLO ACT: WHAT TO DO IF YOU ARE INVITED TO A PARTY WITHOUT A GUEST

A solo invite usually means that the gathering is small and intimate and the guests have been carefully chosen. Perhaps you're part of the balancing act, singles and couples, men and women—so your solo arrival will even out the ratio. Also, don't rule out the inevitable setup: maybe the host has invited a group of singles with the hopes of playing matchmaker. Go with the flow! You'll end up meeting new people and making new friends.

HOW DO YOU ASK IF YOU CAN BRING A GUEST? This is one question that gets posed again and again, and it's a sticky one. Before you even approach this topic with a host, consider the reason why you are asking to bring an extra guest to his or her party, because it had better be a good one! Creating a guest list takes a *ton* of time and effort. Your decision to bring a guest may have a serious and stressful effect on the host, especially when budget is a concern. So before approaching the guest topic, make sure your request isn't frivolous. Check out how our favorite Hollywood party-goers handle it!

"Should I bring one or two hookers (and/or a stripper . . . depends on the kind of party)? As long as you explain how much fun they are and that they are 'easy with the rules' no one will care."

Harry Morton

"Nicely! But be prepared for a no from the hostess."

Dani Janssen

"Most invitations state the obvious. If you aren't sure, simply ask."

Michael Michele

"Be honest and just ask."

Vanna White

"Make sure you say please!"   Hugh Jackman

"Always just reserve for you plus one. Don't bring more. If you reserve for you plus one, then you will have your guest already without having to ask."   Serena Williams

"If you follow the English way of doing things, one just brings whoever one pleases and the hosts have to deal. That's not really cool but there is a 'who cares, life's too short' quality to that attitude."   David Arquette

But if you just don't feel comfortable going alone, ask very nicely if you can bring a guest. If there's a long pause, you'll know the preferred answer is no, and we suggest living with it or turning the invitation down if you just can't bear to accept it. Or fish around a bit to find out the reason for being a solo guest—maybe you know the majority of the guests or the host really wants you to meet someone new. Attending an event without a buffer is an art, especially when you aren't on familiar terms with many of the guests. It takes practice, and most of all, confidence. Prepare yourself for the solo act with these three tips.

1. Speak less, listen more. If you're feeling uncomfortable, ask questions and listen intently to the answers. Learn about the people who fill the room. Remember, everyone loves to talk about themselves! So if you're having trouble chit-chatting, just ask about them.

2. If the conversation is on a subject that you are not well versed in, be content to listen. It's much better to say nothing rather than end up putting yourself on the spot, Because if you give an opinion, you should always be prepared to follow it up. People are bound to question it! And it is surely easier to defend in friendly company than when you are the new face at the table.

3. Avoid polarizing topics like religion and politics. In fact, we recommend avoiding these topics on any first meeting, whether it's a date or a dinner party. Bringing up a religious view can create an awkward moment for all parties involved. Plus, you might rule someone out as a friend because of differing opinions, so you might miss out on forming a new and interesting friendship . . . or love affair!

take note   Listen up, moms and pops, cute as they are, kids *are* considered a plus one. Not only should you call ahead and ask if they're acceptable, but before you do so, think about the type of party. Is it a seated dinner? Better get a babysitter. An afternoon clambake? Now, that's doable.

NO SHOES, NO SHIRT, NO SHINDIG!

Choosing the perfect outfit for a party is always a challenge—especially with little or no directive. There is nothing worse than floating amid a sea of denim in your new (and ever so chic) Cavalli frock, or vice versa. If you receive an invitation that does not explicitly state the dress for the event, ask the host when you RSVP (because you did that, right? Right!).

For a theme party, go all out and dress accordingly, especially if the invitation asks guests to come in costume. If your friend is throwing an eighties bash, swallow your pride and hit the closet to dig out your neon tube socks. Don't be a poor sport about it—you'll ruin the mood of the party and, well, you'll be the only one not having fun with their outfit!

Entertaining has become increasingly casual over the years, resulting in a slew of additions to the dress code like "business casual" or "cocktail casual." Amid the ambiguity of these new terms, even the default "little black dress" has lost its authority. So, even after asking your host what to wear, you may still find yourself struggling to decide between your denim and diamonds. Lucky for you, we translated the attire lingo. Use this chart to find fail-safe outfits for every—and any—occasion.

Cracking the Dress Code

FOR HER

Occasion	Style Solution
Black Tie/Formal	Long dress
Black Tie Optional	Long or three-quarter-length dress
Informal	Always remember that informal means not formal; it does not mean casual. Happy medium? A casual cocktail dress or pants with a killer blouse will do the trick.
Cocktail Casual	Remember that Cavalli frock we mentioned? Perfect.
Business Casual	Enter that amazing Theory pants suit you bought last fall.
Casual	Think pool party or backyard barbecue—denim will always do.

FOR HIM

Occasion	Style Solution
Black Tie	Tuxedo. *Period*.
Black Tie Optional	Just like it sounds—wear a tuxedo if you wish. Otherwise default to a dark suit.
Formal	Dark suit and tie
Informal	Suit. Tie optional.
Cocktail Casual	Sports coat with a collared shirt. Tie optional.
Business Casual	Khakis and a collared shirt. Sports coat and tie optional.
Casual	Denim will always do. Your best pair of jeans paired with a T-shirt will always do the trick.

DRESS TO IMPRESS BY PETER SOM

We asked one of our favorite designers to give us the lowdown on what to wear. Follow his instructions and you're sure to be the belle of the ball!

intimate dinner party

HER   Fitted sweater or a pretty blouse with men's wear–style trousers. Ballerina flats.

HIM   Blazer (only necessary to be worn at entrance and exit), button-down shirt (tucked in, please!), dark rinse jeans, clean sneakers (like low-tops), or brogues (if you can work the no-sock look without getting razzed, go for it).

late night do

HER   Almost anything goes—but only worn with great heels.

HIM   See intimate dinner party above.

beach bash

HER   Sundress with bikini underneath, flat sandals (like Jack Rogers sandals), great straw hat, SPF!

HIM   V-neck non-logo T-shirt or polo shirt, swim trunks, flip-flops, SPF!

brunch

HER   Sundress with cardigan, or loose-fit chiffon blouse with jeans. Flats.

HIM   Polo shirt, plain front khakis, clean sneakers. Optional dark rinse jean jacket or other light jacket.

cocktails

HER   Fabulous cocktail dress, those sexy heels, and a bold cuff or earrings.

HIM   Slim-fit suit with shirt (use your own judgment about wearing a tie), shined brogues.

chic tip   Do not wear a hat to a party (with the exception of the obvious backyard BBQ or any event by a large body of water). In other words, unless the event is a beach bash or poolside soiree, leave the baseball cap at home.

FASHION POLICE

If you do commit a style crime the most important thing to remember is to avoid drawing attention to your error of dress. Your preoccupation with it will make others zero in on it as well. Act confidently and add self deprecating humor as needed.

We leave you with these parting tips:

- It is always safer to overdress. You can always dress down but you can never dress up.

- Be yourself. If you hate wearing a bow tie or tuxedo, wear your own version of black-tie. Many men wear a gorgeous designer black suit with a snazzy tie. You don't want to look like a penguin, but this will keep your look within reason. Being creative and yourself does not mean the worn-out cargo pants you wear daily are acceptable.

- If an invitation notes that a certain type of dress is "preferred" or "optional," you can dress slightly less formally, but not casually.

- Don't stand out. In other words, that hot pink leopard-printed skin-tight gown? Leave it in the closet. Keep it simple, elegant, and fabulous.

- When the invitation notes a particular color, like Oprah's Black and White Ball, that means guests should wear black or white. Don't decide this is the occasion to buck the tradition and wear red. Formal and older hosts recommend that if you don't want to follow the dress code, then stay home.

- Costume parties: Wear one! Don't be the dud in your everyday wear. Go all out, and make the party twice the fun.

COMING AND GOING

Arrivals and departures are often a source of angst for an attendee. When do I come? How long do I stay? How do I make an early exit? Where exactly is the line between "fashionably late" and just plain late? Entrances and exits must be strategic and calculated. While deciding when to arrive and leave is often dependent on the type of event, it is also relatively formulaic. Here are the basic principles of coming and going:

- **Don't arrive at a party unannounced** If you decide the day before the event that you want to attend, but did not RSVP, do not show up at a party without first having called the host. Apologize for not having responded in a timely manner and express your interest in attending. At this point, it is up to your host to say yea or nay. At larger events, a finalized list is usually given to whoever is tasked with manning the door. A quick phone call will save you the embarrassment of showing up only to be turned away. Likewise, your host has enough to tend to, and frankly no time to address your causing a stir at the door.

- **Don't be the early bird** A time is stated on an invitation for a reason. Your host will resent it (no matter how gracious he/she may act). And, for your own sake, nothing takes the glamour out of a party like arriving to a host scrambling in her slippers, still trying to find the perfect place for her peonies.

- Don't be the first to arrive and don't be the last to leave.

TIMING, IT REALLY IS EVERYTHING

As we said before, your arrival must be tactical. An arrival strategy must be based on the type of event you are attending.

- Always bear in mind, however, that hosts get nervous when people are late. For fluid gatherings like open-house style events, your arrival can be flexible. Do, however, arrive no later than an hour before the party is set to end.

- For a seated dinner, or events with a specific program/agenda, never arrive more than fifteen minutes after the scheduled start time.

- For any other type of event with a specific start time, we suggest arriving fifteen to twenty minutes after the party is set to begin. This window allows you to stake your claim on prime real estate (aka the coveted couch), greet the host/guest of honor, get a drink, and settle in. Then you can sit back and enjoy your unobstructed view of who's coming in the door.

- If you are running late, especially to a smaller event, call your host to alert them and provide an ETA.

- And because we knew you'd ask, if we had to approximate it, fashionably late would be fifteen minutes.

YOU'VE ARRIVED . . . NOW WHAT?

- Greet the host or guest of honor immediately upon arriving. It is courteous to find and thank them before making your rounds.

- If you have to leave early, don't tell the host now. If you know in advance that you will have to make an early exit, alert your host when you RSVP. This is especially important for a seated dinner. Simply tell your host upon RSVP'ing that you have to duck out before dessert.

- If you are running late, then call ahead, especially in the cases of smaller parties or seated dinners. The plan of attack should be two-fold: first, call your host and let them know you are running late, and second, assure them that they should start without you (even if you truly can't bear the thought of missing the crab cake appetizer). Face it, it's likely that the host is tending to other guests and may not answer, but you called and that's courteous.

EXITS ARE AT THE FRONT AND BACK OF THE CABIN

Even the classiest of soirees tend to have a guest who stays just a tad too long. Like arrivals, deciding when to leave is also dependent, in part, on the type of event. An invitation may not always include a specific end time. This, however, does not give you license to assume that means it is an all-night bash. There are certain benchmarks to note in crafting your exit strategy.

- If the invitation states an end time, you must be out by that time unless the host is (genuinely) insisting that people stay.

- At a seated dinner, you can assume it is safe to depart forty-five minutes after dessert is served.

- Other events, say a casual cocktail party or an open house, are trickier. For an open house, we suggest that you stay a minimum of twenty minutes (although thirty wouldn't kill you) simply so as not to seem like your appearance is completely obligatory.

- Don't engage in a long conversation with your host at the door. Remember that your host has other guests to tend to and save the gossip for a later chat.

YOU DON'T HAVE TO GO HOME, BUT YOU CAN'T STAY HERE

The most important thing to remember in determining your departure is to stay attuned to social cues. Every guest should note the five telltale signs that a party is over and heed the cue to leave.

1. Lights up

2. Music down

3. Bar closed

4. Food not being served/replenished

5. Host is cleaning up/staff is breaking down

LIGHTS, CAMERA, ACTION! THE ROLE OF THE GUEST

As we said, the guest has a specific function and an important role at any event. Aside from the compulsory RSVP, dressing the part, and making a well-thought-out arrival and departure, there are certain implicit laws that govern guests while at a party. There are some basic dos and don'ts that will keep you on your host's good side while partying the night away.

- Helping hand Do offer to help your host, especially if there is no staff on hand. But don't insist if your host declines.

- Party animal Don't bring your pet (even if Lulu Flynn is your token arm candy) unless it is a canine-specific bash or unless you've cleared it with your host in advance.

- Electronic etiquette We always suggest leaving phones, pagers, BlackBerrys, Treos, or any other communication device on silent or vibrate, especially at small, intimate events. However, don't panic. If you absolutely cannot bear the thought of parting with your BlackBerry, at the very least, make sure that you have it on silent or vibrate during the party. Try to avoid answering your phone at the party. If you must take the call, excuse yourself and go somewhere private. There are few things more grating than someone chatting on the telephone at a social gathering.

take note   As dog owners, this is a pet peeve of ours that we need to put out there. No one should touch your dog unless they ask first. Observe the same etiquette as with someone's child (we assume you know that picking up someone's child is absolutely a no-no!). In the case of our fur-coated pals, the dog may not be friendly, it may be frightened of strangers, or maybe the owner just doesn't like it. Be respectful; ask before stroking the pup's belly. And the same restraint goes for parents: don't allow your kids to run and pet a dog. That's how accidents can happen.

DIFFUSING DISASTERS

We've covered just about every situation you might encounter as a guest, but there are some unexpected situations that come up. Take into account how we handle each of the problems below, because no matter what the situation entails, the correct way to deal with it is usually the same: be polite and don't make a scene.

problem **A big presentation just landed in your lap,** minutes before you were slipping away to get all dolled up for the big party tonight. You're looking at an all-nighter, meaning you're not going to make it to the party that's starting in fifteen minutes. Do you call with a last-minute cancellation?

solution **Our first impulse is to say, without a doubt, yes.** But first, take into consideration how many guests are invited. Is it a two-hundred-plus party? In that case, the host might not even realize you didn't make it, but if it's a small party of twenty, you'd better pick up the phone *tout de suite*! In the case of a huge gala, you might call your date or best friend to pass along the unfortunate news, and even if the news is passed along in that manner, don't count out speaking to the host. Call the next day and explain your situation.

problem **Scent overload.** You're enjoying a dinner at your boss's home but his wife has decorated the place with highly perfumed flowers that are killing your allergies. Your nose is running and your head is pounding. And you've sneezed so many times people have run out of clever comebacks.

s o l u t i o n   **Whenever you have an issue such as this,** whether it be an overpowering scent from flowers or candles, or you're freezing under the blast of an air-conditioner, it's best to mention it to the host. Don't make a scene, simply mention to the host that you're sneezing up a storm due to the gardenias and ask to move your seat. Same goes for a chilly blast from the a/c, or when you're roasting next to a heat lamp. Your host wants you to be comfortable, so speak up! Don't sit there and sneeze, freeze, or sweat. Politely ask the host to help out. Or better yet, if there is staff on hand ask them to turn the air down or the heat up, or move the flowers to another spot.

p r o b l e m   **While telling a particularly animated story,** you fling your arm out and send Merlot flying across the tablecloth and your neighbor's white polo shirt. Oops!

s o l u t i o n   **Foremost, issue an apology and offer the soiled party a napkin.** Aid in the cleaning and volunteer to pay for any necessary dry cleaning after the fact. The offer to pick up the cleaning tab or necessary repairs should be a conversation held in private after the meal. Most good hosts will refuse your offer. In this case, send a token of regret to your host the next day (like a replacement tablecloth). If your faux pas goes down at a restaurant, discreetly signal a server for help.

p r o b l e m   **Breakdown!** You just sat down to converse with a pal when the chair beneath you collapsed. Not fun and definitely embarrassing. What now?

s o l u t i o n **No one likes to be in this situation.** Not long ago, a friend of ours was at a dinner party and when he sat down on an antique rocking chair, it crumbled beneath him. Not fun! In a situation like this, whether it's a table, chair, or wine glass, the only thing you can do is apologize and make a light joke—the latter depending on how the host is handling the situation. If it's an expensive piece of furniture or a Baccarat glass, you should offer to pay for it. And, as a host, unless the guest was injured you must overlook it and assure the guest there's nothing to worry about. These things happen and if you are worried about breaking your fine china, then don't use it.

p r o b l e m **Bad Lulu!** She made a mistake at your host's home, right smack in the middle of the living room.

s o l u t i o n **If you're a house guest at anyone's home** and your pet goes to the bathroom, you must always, no ifs, ands, or buts, offer to pay for cleaning. No matter what the situation, your pet made the mistake—now fix it. Apologize profusely and help the host with cleanup. If no one catches Lulu in the poopy act, you may be tempted to avoid the confrontation by cleaning it up and pretending it didn't happen. But doing this has ramifications; the next time a dog comes to visit it may smell the remainder and decide to mark its territory. It's a chain reaction! So just 'fess up, it's the right thing to do.

What Is Your Biggest Party Fear, Disaster, or Embarrassing Moment?

Tossing and turning after last night's party? Maybe you had too much to drink, hit on a taken man or woman, or told the worst joke ever. You're not the only one who worries about doing the wrong thing at a social affair.

> "Committing a major party faux pas like sleeping with the host's significant other."   Harry Morton

EATING, DRINKING, AND GENERAL MERRIMENT

Quite simply, eat and drink responsibly. Food and drink, while an integral party element, should not be your priority. This is not the era of Roman excess and no vomitoriums will be provided, nor should you ever need one! By all means indulge, but pace yourself.

1. DO NOT GET DRUNK Do not get drunk. Do not get drunk. There is nothing more tawdry, tacky, and miserable than a guest who is wasted, hammered, sloshed, plastered, tanked, pissed, or any version of too-much!

2. DO NOT ARRIVE AT A PARTY HUNGRY! Pigging out like you've been fasting for a week is not appetizing.

3. ALWAYS USE COASTERS You do not want to be the guest who leaves a water stain on your host's antique teak chest. If a coaster is not provided, hold your drink in your hand.

4. DON'T DROP YOUR CIGARETTE BUTTS! Put them in an ashtray, please. If none is provided, then ask for one. If you must light up, go outside. But please, please, whatever you do, don't try to create a makeshift ashtray out of a potted plant, wad of tinfoil, cocktail glass, or anything inside the house. Ever.

5. BE FRIENDLY, MINGLE, AND HAVE FUN It is the host's duty to make introductions, but after that the ball is in your court. Don't monopolize the host or follow them around. You don't want to be the guest who the host feels they have to entertain or babysit. Make an effort to engage in conversation with the other guests but don't monopolize one guest's time. Rather, try to meet and mingle with as many people as possible. We suggest standing near the buffet or bar to meet people.

6. DON'T BE DORA THE EXPLORER Keep to the areas specifically decorated for the party and use the designated restroom. And, however tempting to do so, avoid snooping through your host's medicine cabinet or bedroom. I mean, really, what could you find that would be so interesting?

7. GET A ROOM! We're happy you found love, truly we are. But please, don't even think about hooking up in any of the bedrooms, or for that matter, don't make out like two horny high school kids. *Puh-leeze.*

Always hold your drink in your left hand so you can shake hands with your right.

STARRY-EYED SURPRISE

Omigod, is that Charlize Theron? Get it under control, missy. Attending a celebrity event can be the coolest thing, but it can also set you up for a big kick in the butt from a security guard if you misbehave. Follow these guidelines and you'll continue to make the cut!

* No photographs

* No autographs

* Avoid comments like "I swear I recognize you from somewhere" or things of that nature because chances are, you do. At other parties such questions are fine but questions like that may seem desperate and phony at parties with heavy celebrity quotient.

DIALOGUE DECORUM

1. Speak up! But not too loud . . . Verbal blunders can bring a party to a standstill and nothing spoils the mood like two guests embroiled in an aggressive debate about the current state of politics.

2. Party conversation should be light. Generally speaking, avoid controversial topics like religion and politics. Broach such sticky subject matter and you may find that your conversation with that charming doctor you've been chatting up suddenly takes a turn for the worse.

3. Shy away from posing personal questions or any questions about things like age and income. A party is never the proper forum for such matters. Besides, your seemingly innocent question about the state of one's relationship may lead to an emotional rant about a messy divorce.

4. Most important, refrain from talking badly about the host, other guests, or anything about the party. Save your critique of the catering for post-party discussion.

5. Refrain from whispering, yawning, complaining, or doing anything that implies boredom or otherwise isolates you from the other guests. And please, save the ego-stroking for another outing.

6. Keep it clean. Sorry to say, but your mama was right: no one loves a potty mouth. Leave the four-letter words out of any and every conversation.

chic tip   Who said chivalry is dead? Guys, when you are introduced to a woman, *stand up.* Take it from us, you'll win one serious Eagle Scout merit badge.

Who Is That?

Sometimes you draw a blank. You're standing in front of a guy who you know you know, but his name has just slipped your mind. Cover up your brain slip by bringing someone over, whose name you *do* know, and say, "You know Elizabeth, right?" The nameless guy will naturally extend his hand and introduce himself. Problem solved.

MONEY TALKS

Gratuity is not strictly the concern of the host. There are certain times when a guest will be expected to tip as well. Tips are accepted when . . .

- Valet is provided Just like any other time you valet your car, the valet is rendering a service. If you would normally tip, this instance is no exception. Do not assume that the host has prepaid gratuities. A couple of dollars will do.

- There is an open bar Let's put it this way: if there is a tip jar on the bar, slipping in a couple of singles during the night may help ensure that your drink stays strong.

- Or a cash bar A cash bar functions like any other bar. Tip as you would on a Wednesday at your favorite watering hole.

- The waitstaff is super attentive Generally guests are not expected to tip in this situation. And quite frankly, presenting a

tip in front of other guests may make them uncomfortable. If
there are servers who go out of their way for you and you feel
compelled to slip them some cash, send some the next day with
a note expressing your thanks.

- Coat check Always tip the person handling the coat check a
  dollar or two, depending on the number of coats or packages. If
  you do happen to have packages you need stored away, fork
  over a few extra bucks for their help.

SAYING THANK YOU

A gracious guest always thanks the host properly. One should
always, always toast the host at the event to say thanks for planning
such an amazing, wonderful, thoughtful, incredible afternoon or
evening. And follow that praise with a thank-you note. Yes, thank-you
notes are a must and, call us old-fashioned, but handwritten is
always best. Try to reserve e-mail thank-you notes for larger, more
impersonal events. But even then, a handwritten note never hurts.
Send a note as soon as possible after the event—we suggest sending
the note within two days.

chic tip   A nice touch is to enclose a photograph that was taken
at the event inside the thank-you note.

The New Way to Date

Facebook is a new social networking tool for high school students, college students, and other people organized by city. It has changed the way people connect and interact and includes a "mini-feed" section where your every move is tracked and displayed to your network of friends. It tracks new photos of you, your personal status, and most important, who you have become new friends with. Unlike MySpace, Facebook is a much more organized and well-respected social networking site. Some people may be creeped out by the mini-feed, but only people who are my friends can view it.

There are some crazy phenoms about Facebook. For example, instead of giving someone's phone number, an exchange of names takes place and then one or the other may send a "friend request." Now the two can find out what they have in common and get to know each other. People can write on each other's "wall" once they are friends—basically a public display of short e-mails. It's a great way to flirt. If people are serious, for one dollar, a virtual gift can be sent for all to see as well. It is almost as special as a real gift because now everyone can see how two people are connected.

In fact, some people think you aren't real friends until you are officially friends on Facebook.

PICTURE PERFECT

Let's face it, we're not all supermodels. Posing for a photograph can be daunting, stressful, and downright depressing (especially when you're always the double-chinned guest in the post-party pics). Many people just hate the sight of a lens pointed in their direction, especially the camera shy. So how do Hollywood starlets manage to look picture perfect at all times? Renowned photographers Tierney Gearon; Patrick McMullan, creator of www.PatrickMcMullan.com; Jeff Vespa of WireImage; and Myriam Santos-Kayda, photographer and director, reveal the star-polished secrets on looking great in every photograph.

chic tip If you don't want to be in a picture with someone, for whatever reason, the surest way to keep that photo out of circulation is to close your eyes.

what angle produces the most flattering photograph?

MYRIAM SANTOS-KAYDA "One good trick is to have subjects turn their hips at a slight angle, even if their shoulders are facing the camera, to make them look leaner."

TIERNEY GEARON "If you are fat, stand behind someone and cuddle into them. If you have a double chin, stretch your neck up and keep your chin slightly down."

JEFF VESPA "One foot forward and shoulders back, but you really need to figure out your best angle. Practice in the mirror and research old photos."

how should you distribute your weight to appear the thinnest?

JEFF VESPA "Suck in your stomach and stand up straight. Keep your shoulders back and chest out. This will elongate you and make your clothes lie better."

TIERNEY GEARON "Always stand three-quarters angle body square. Hips three-quarters."

MYRIAM SANTOS-KAYDA "Have the subject turn the hips away from the camera, and put the weight on the back leg, and drop the back shoulder a bit."

what is the best position to have in a group photograph?

PATRICK McMULLAN "Be ready. Don't hold up group pics by futzing around."

JEFF VESPA "The middle. The camera can cut you off if you are on an end, plus the lens can distort people on the outside of the frame."

what should you wear (or not wear) when you know you are going to be photographed?

MYRIAM SANTOS-KAYDA "This one is difficult, depends on the group and depends on the lighting, which is everything."

PATRICK McMULLAN "Depends on the occasion and body type. Solids are best."

JEFF VESPA "Bold colors look the best in photos. Make sure bra straps aren't showing. Also make sure you always wear undergarments because the flash acts like X-ray vision and can reveal more than you intend."

what are your tips for looking great in every photo?

PATRICK MCMULLAN "Be happy someone wants your pic. Don't be negative, it's fun."

TIERNEY GEARON "The most important thing to do when someone is taking your photo is number one, do not talk. And number two, make sure you find someone to focus on that makes you laugh or feel good. When you are relaxed, you look beautiful. The trick to a great photographer is one that makes the subject feel beautiful."

JEFF VESPA "Don't hold a drink or cigarette. Make sure your makeup is always touched up and do a dress check in the restroom every half hour to forty-five minutes. Always make sure you have a compact in your bag. And make sure you always stop in front of the WireImage photographer!"

HOW DO YOU CRASH A PARTY?

There comes a time when you absolutely must be at a particular party. No, it's not the most respectful move to crash a party, but let's face it, crashing happens! But before you decide to brazenly waltz up to a private dinner party of six at your ex-boyfriend's house, heed this piece of advice: there is a time and place for everything—especially crashing parties! Big, splashy events where you will easily blend in is the kind of party we're talking about. Anything smaller, so not okay!

"I am an Aussie; we crash a party and we stay until the sun comes up." Hugh Jackman

"You crash a party by just showing up and looking posh. Act like you belong there. Be sexy, not slutty, and have fun!!! And get as many free drinks as you can!" Serena Williams

"You don't. If one has not been invited, then one shouldn't arrive unannounced. It's classless." Michael Michele

"Couldn't tell you. Would feel too uncomfortable doing something like that. Only go where you are welcome." Harry Morton

"Dressed hot with Christian Louboutin shoes." Molly Sims

"No one should! But if you must, then dress in costume and say you're the entertainment sent by a friend. (You'd better know how to sing, dance, or tell jokes!) Since the host didn't set aside time for unexpected entertainment, chances are you'll never have to perform anyway, so remove the outer costume and in your regular clothes, you'll be mingling with the guests."

Dani Janssen

HOW DO YOU MAKE AN EARLY EXIT?

There are times when being the last guest standing is the last thing you want to happen. Maybe you are stressed out at work, tired, have other plans, or just don't want to be there! But leaving early can be a tough move to pull off. Check out these party pros' plan of attack for slipping out.

"Scoot out the back door."

Vanna White

"Prepare yourself. Give yourself an appropriate time, and if possible inform your host/hostess that you'll be leaving early."

Michael Michele

"Just excuse yourself in a nice way and say you have to wake up early in the morning."

Serena Williams

"Violent and explosive. Complain of diarrhea, it is the best excuse. No one ever questions or tries to talk you out of leaving."

Harry Morton

"Act like you're going to the bathroom."

Molly Sims

"Quietly! Call the next day with your excuse and it better be a good one."

Dani Janssen

six

THE GALLANT GOURMET

forks, knives, and spoons . . . all in order!

HOSTING A SEATED DINNER PARTY or any party where food is a primary focus, can bring up a slew of unique elements for a host to consider, like what do you do if someone is vegan? How do you decide where to seat everyone, especially if two people don't like each other? Where does the wine glass go, the salad fork? Relax. We've got the answers. This chapter schools hosts and guests alike on the rules of dining decorum to ensure that you handle your next dinner party, whether hosting or attending, with finesse.

DINING DECORUM

TICK-TOCK The timing of a dinner party will be different than a casual cocktail party or charity event. The obvious time, under normal circumstances, is between 7 and 8 p.m. But when selecting the time you must take into consideration the guests and the occasion. For example, when planning a dinner for co-workers, aim for 6 to 6:30 p.m. so people can go directly from work and are able to get home to their families and significant others (and yes, that includes their TiVo) at a reasonable hour. Early dinners are also an option if you're going to a concert, movie, play, or anything that begins later on. The same thinking applies to late dinners. Consider scheduling at 9:30 or 10 p.m. after a fashion show, gallery opening, movie screening, or any event that occurs earlier in the evening.

THE CENTER OF ATTENTION We love a brilliant bouquet as much as the next, just be sure to choose a floral centerpiece that will not obstruct the guests' view. Try an arrangement of hedged roses (or any flower you love), floating gardenias and candles in a crystal bowl, or place a stem at each person's plate, whatever inspires you—just keep it low. This keeps the table pretty and ensures your best bud can make eyes at the cute boy she has been waiting months to meet.

take note   The type of event determines the style of the dinner party. A seated dinner is great before heading out to a movie, or a light three-course meal is just the ticket after a fashion show or art opening. For example, we recently threw a dinner party for Fergie after her concert at The Palms. The scene was casual and very informal with a smorgasbord of sushi and upscale diner-chic food trays passed through the crowd. Because, let's face it, with all the energy pumping after shaking our humps, none of us wanted to sit down to a five-course French dinner!

Cocktail Tips

- Always keep the length of cocktail hour to no more than one hour.

- Don't forget the appetizers! Yes, dinner is coming but people will have growling bellies, so give them something to curb—and stimulate—their appetite.

CRAFTING THE MENU Hosts tend to think a dinner party requires extravagant, impressive food, and that's great—if you're a five-star chef. Here are our foolproof methods for creating a menu that will leave guests wanting another helping.

- Select items that are simple and easy and then give them a gourmet twist, either in preparation or presentation.

- Always serve a salad. That way if someone has diet restrictions—whether they are on a diet, vegetarian, or just super picky, they will have *something* to eat.

- If you're giving diners a choice, always offer a meat, chicken, and fish dish and serve a carb (potatoes, bread, rice, pasta) and a vegetable with all the choices. Sure, you can elect to serve only a rack of lamb, but some people may not like it, so that's where side dishes play an important role by giving picky eaters something to fill up on.

- Go for the bird. Serving chicken is a budget-saving option and there are some delicious and simple preparations. Get out your cookbooks and start searching.

- Never make a recipe for the first time at a dinner party. Always, always do a test run or better yet, go with a dish that is tried and true.

- Know your crowd. If it's an adventurous group, you can go out on a limb but be sure to serve a palate pleaser along with your newfangled recipe. In fact, we recommend going with a favorite every time so it becomes your signature. For example, Dani

Janssen always serves her famous monkey bread and guests clamor for it.

- Better yet, choose dishes that are simple to make but that can be served in a gourmet manner. For example, macaroni and cheese can be served in individual ramekins; hamburgers can be dressed up with a blue cheese crumble, Applewood bacon, caramelized onion, and so on. Get creative with those old favorites!

- Offer nonalcoholic options. If a toast is on tap, chill a bottle of sparkling grape juice for the nondrinkers to pop with the bubbly.

- If guests don't mention allergies or make special requests, ask about any dietary restrictions. Guests may feel uncomfortable bringing such things up, so alleviate pressure and ask them when they RSVP.

HELPING HAND Many hosts hire professional servers, bartenders, kitchen staff, and so on when throwing a dinner party. We can't agree with this more. Not only does a hired staff make your job easier, it adds a formal element to the get-together. Hired staff doesn't have to be a professional catering team. If you're working within a budget, consider hiring your niece, nephew, your best friend's daughter, or the neighbor kids to help out. It's the perfect penny-saving option for a casual gathering.

Whether you've hired one person to assist in the kitchen or a full catering staff, be sure to brief them on every detail. Hold a meeting beforehand to explain exactly what, when, and how you would like guests to be served. Emphasize your expectations by posting instructions in clear view *and* hand a copy to each member of the staff at the beginning of your pre-party meeting.

 Always sample the food in advance before hiring a catering service, even if they come highly recommended. Set up a tasting so you can sample menu items for both taste and presentation.

LARA AND ELIZABETH'S TIPS FOR SERVING SUCCESS

Follow our serving tips for a heavenly evening.

1. Greet guests at the door with a signature cocktail. At Harrison & Shriftman events, we always have servers stationed at the entry so guests immediately feel welcome.

2. As soon as the first guest arrives, begin serving appetizers. Don't make them wait for five other people to arrive before breaking out the food—get the party started right away.

3. Pick up dirty glasses or plates immediately. Not only does doing this make cleanup easier at the end of the night, but it keeps the party from looking like a frat house party!

4. Pay attention to the appearance of placed appetizers. There's nothing more unappetizing than a dish of lumpy, gray guacamole in the middle of the table. Make sure dishes are replenished frequently throughout the party.

5. Make sure the servers understand what they are serving. Not only should they be able to pronounce the name of the dish, but they must be able to explain the ingredients in detail. Trust us, guests will ask, "What's that?" when pointing to something as simple as a cone of fries dusted in garlic and herbs.

6. Decide how you want your servers to be dressed and have the outfit match the event. There is nothing worse than a group of tuxedo-clad servers running around a western-themed bash. So at a beach party, outfit servers in khaki pants and a white T-shirt, or at a dressy dinner party dress 'em up in black pants and a white button-down. If you're throwing an Indian dinner, have the staff wear saris so the theme is carried through. These touches make your party stand out. Just keep in mind, whatever fashion you dictate, keep the look universal.

7. On the invitation, clearly indicate the time span for cocktail hour and dinnertime. For example, state: cocktails from 7 to 8, dinner at 8 p.m. sharp. This allows people to plan accordingly. They know arriving any time between 7 and 8 is acceptable but anything after 8 is gauche.

SIZE MATTERS

Rectangular, square, round, one long table, U-shape . . . Let's face it, there are a ton of options when it comes to the table shape.

- At Harrison & Shriftman, we prefer round tables for every size gathering, whether it's for ten or one hundred. The circular shape is the best setting for conversing, and if you have more than one table, grouping them close together makes it possible for people to join conversations at neighboring tables as well. When throwing dinner parties, Lara and Elizabeth prefer to use a larger, six-top table set for eight. It makes for an intimate setting by bringing people closer together and when someone doesn't show up, the table doesn't suffer from empty chair syndrome.

- Another option is one long table; this is best for parties of twenty people and less. If you have twenty or so guests, the length dilutes conversation because realistically, people only speak to the two people next to them and across from them. And when someone wants to talk to someone some thirty people down, they end up shouting and all the gabbing in between comes to a halt.

- Don't seat any table with fewer than six people. Six, eight, ten, and twelve are the norms. And never, ever sit a table with two or four people. Not only is it depressing for the guests, but it makes the guests feel like they are on the D-list. A large event of one hundred or more may end up with one or two tables that are suffering from a rash of no-shows, and in such cases squeeze them together or add people to the other tables in the room.

- Depending on the size of your table, generally six to eight people can be seated comfortably at one table. If you have eight-plus guests, we suggest using two tables. But beware of the bureaucracy; the host's table will always be viewed as the best place to sit. If you use two tables, place your co-host at the other table.

take note   Don't pack your guests around a table like sardines; intimate and cozy is the key. While we are fans of seating people close together, we aren't implying that you should squash eight people around a four-top. You want guests to be comfortable, so make sure that the table can accommodate everyone's legs, elbows, and place settings.

MUSICAL CHAIRS

A host must be fluent in the unspoken language of seating arrangements, and believe us, there are times when it's harder to decide where to seat someone than it is to order off a French menu! In addition, you also have to tend to guests' egos when crafting your table. No matter how much thought you put into your six tables of ten, inevitably someone will rush over to you complaining that they can't possibly sit at table two because they don't know a soul. Meanwhile, two guests will arrive who didn't RSVP while another will call and cancel at the last minute. Not to mention the encounters with ego. People always infer a pecking order when it comes to seated tables. Someone who you agonized over where to place and finally placed at table six is going to think table one is the best table in the house and decide she's been snubbed. And the mayhem begins.

Clearly, seating can be a nightmare, but it is also an incredible tool when orchestrating a dinner. The arrangement can avert awkward situations, encourage new relationships, or make the whole night flop. No pressure there, huh? Place cards immediately make the evening more formal and puts you in charge of the situation. In some groups, you may not want to leave your guests to their own devices, while in other situations freedom of choice is just what the crowd needs. In the case of the latter, letting guests seat themselves is less stressful for the host. Just take into consideration the crowd before ditching place cards; if it's a free-for-all crowd you won't have to worry about empty chairs. Before you decide on seating arrangements versus none, take into consideration these five points.

1.   BE STRATEGIC The seating arrangement makes or breaks a party. It sets the tone and establishes the dynamic of the meal. That being said, each guest's position should make them feel like they have the best seat in the house.

2.   CONVERSATION IS KEY Create a table that is conducive to conversation. Place guests next to someone you are confident they will be able to chat with over multiple courses.

3.   WHO SITS WHERE? Okay, so you want to get everyone

chatting. But making this happen is not as simple as it sounds. Simply put, you have to decide where each person should sit and who should sit next to them. Customarily, the host sits at the end of the table and the co-host at the opposite end. If the dinner is in someone's honor, the guest of honor sits next to the host. If you are having more than one table, you may want to consider having a host committee and then having each host head a table.

4. MIX AND MATCH Keep in mind that a creative blend of people facilitates interesting conversation and promotes new relationships. Think about the table arrangement in terms of casting a movie. Consider everyone's interests, hobbies, professions, and recent travels and then mix it up. It's sure to be a blockbuster hit!

5. KEEPIN' IT FAMILIAR Attempt to place each guest near someone they know. This prevents guests from sitting down to a slew of new people. There's nothing tougher than making small talk the entire evening. If a few people at the table know each other they will immediately get the conversation flowing. Just don't sit them right next to each other or they may ignore the rest of the group. Sprinkle them throughout the table so everyone gets involved. Another idea is to separate couples. Splitting them up makes them more likely to engage with other guests. Time-honored tradition dictates that you should alternate males and females all the way around the table. We are all for this, but only when and if it makes sense for your gathering.

take note   Seating has been a source of drama throughout history!
The 1815 Congress of Vienna addressed the fiery
disputes that arose among diplomats angling for the
most prestigious spots. In order to establish order, the
Congress of Vienna stated the rule that ambassadors
were to be ranked according to the length of time they
had held their posts—whether they represented
superpowers or tiny principalities.

chic tip   Seat left-handed guests at the end of either side of the
table where they are less likely to knock their neighbor.

THE SCIENCE OF SEATING

It's time to get down to business. Seating can be a stressful and
puzzling process, but there is a method to the madness.

1. Make a list of all the people you have invited. Separate the men
   and women if you plan to go with boy-girl seating.

2. Get a floor plan of the venue or make your own if one is not
   available or you are doing the event at home.

3. Decide on the shape and number of tables you will need to
   accommodate the guests.

4. Make a diagram of the room by drawing the tables. Consider

how close you want each table to be to other tables and the flow of the entire room.

5. Number each table.

6. Enlarge the diagram and laminate it.

7. Take round Avery labels and write each person's name. If you are seating people according to sex, consider using different colors, red for women, blue for men.

8. Start sticking! Just don't press the labels down permanently; adhere them lightly so you can move people around until the arrangement is perfect, or change the seating if someone cancels.

9. Check the master list—again. Make sure you didn't forget anyone!

10. Photocopy the diagram once it's finalized.

chic tip   A creative way to seat people is to name the tables after flowers, people, cities, states, countries, or anything that matches the mood of your dinner.

take note   Always have extra chairs and place settings on hand, so if that unexpected guest shows up, you have somewhere to seat them.

Lara is a stickler for seating arrangements, especially when it comes to parties of ten or more. And while parties of six or eight don't necessarily need to be seated, before throwing place cards to the wind, think about what you want out of the evening. Maybe you're trying to play matchmaker. If the couple sits at opposite ends, the love connection may never happen!

Place cards

Photo credit: Myriam Santos

PLACE CARD PROTOCOL

Place cards should be used at any meal with a seating arrangement, because it makes things easier. That way no one will be fighting over the coveted seat next to yours truly. If you decide to ditch the formal place cards, you're not off duty. Guests will look to the host to facilitate where they should sit. Make a few suggestions or tell everyone to just grab a seat. Be aware; if someone looks unsure or awkward, step up and make a suggestion.

So how do you script the cards? We prefer to include the guest's first name only. If two guests share the same first name, include a last initial as well. For formal events, you may choose to include first and last names. And our last piece of advice? Make the cards well in advance! Don't try to print them out twenty minutes before the dinner begins. That is a disaster in the making.

Write a special note to guests inside the place card, whether it's as simple as "Happy you're here!" or more eloquent, like a memorable phrase, line, or quote that holds meaning for you both.

Put guests' names on both sides of the place cards. This is such a great ice breaker at tables where not everyone knows your name. It prevents awkward pauses (like when you want that guy across the table to pass the butter but you can't remember his name) and keeps the conversation flowing, plus, it makes the introduction thing go all that much faster!

take note   Always purchase extra place cards, especially if you are having a calligrapher do them or you're printing them yourself. Inevitably, a mistake will be made and another will be needed. A messed up place card can ruin the whole table! If you printed them yourself, save the font and dimensions so if you need to run off another at the last minute it's easily done.

PERFECTLY PLACED

Setting a table can be daunting. Suddenly you're caught up in a debate of where to put the wine glass and whether or not you need chargers. But before you subscribe to your grandmother's way of doing it, keep this in mind: traditional place settings are the kind of traditions that are in need of an update. It's important to know and understand the traditional table, but we are huge proponents of creating unique table settings. Think of it this way: feel free to tap into the old charm school rules but be ready and willing to give them a modern twist.

Place setting by Tiffany & Co., menu by Bernard Maisner, at Hotel Bel-Air   Photo credit: John Shearer/WireImage

1. THE RULE OF THUMB Place settings are dictated by the menu. If you are only serving three courses, then you will need less gear than if you are doing a seven-course meal.

2. BUCK CONVENTION Don't include extraneous utensils just because you think it's required. Leave the soup spoon in the drawer if you're not ladling it up! The spoon confuses guests, clutters the table, and just doesn't make sense.

3. APPEARANCE IS EVERYTHING A perfectly set table is fouled by dirty dishware or mismatched utensils. Make sure to use matching silverware and glassware that is smudge free. This goes for your stainless steel and silver as well. Get polishing!

PRINCIPLES OF PLACE SETTING

Glasses should be arranged in order of descending height and placed at the top right of the dinner plate, above the knives and spoons with the water glass closest to the plate. At casual or semicasual functions, separate glasses for red wine, white wine, and water are not necessary. You can either replace the glasses when switching from white to red or if you are offering both, go with a simple wine glass that is acceptable for either.

The traditional wine glass has had a makeover. There are so many choices in glassware, stemless, decorated, and more. If you are stylizing the table feel free to mix it up. Use a stemless Reidel for the red wine and a goblet for water. Just have extras on hand so that if someone wants to switch from white to red, you don't have to run to the kitchen and start washing.

Dos and Don'ts

Do serve water in pitchers

Do offer nonalcoholic beverages

Don't place individual water bottles on table

Don't place cans or bottles on the table. Pour into a cocktail glass and serve.

the basic or informal place setting

The forks are placed to the left of the plate. The dinner fork, the larger of the two forks, is used for the main course; the smaller fork is used for a salad or appetizer. The forks are arranged according to when you need to use them, following an "outside-in" order. If the small fork is needed for an appetizer or a salad served before the main course, then it is placed on the left (outside) of the dinner fork; if the salad is served after the main course, then the small fork is placed to the right (inside) of the dinner fork, next to the plate.

The dinner knife is set immediately to the right of the plate. If the main course is meat, a steak knife can take the place of the dinner knife. Knife blades always face inward, toward the center of the plate. Spoons for appetizer/soup are placed to the right of the knife/knives. Napkins sit to the left of the fork or are on the plate when guests are seated.

Other dishes and utensils are optional, depending on what is being served. Whenever possible, we encourage bringing dishes out as the courses are served to keep as few dishes as possible on the table at any given time. The dishes may include any of those below.

THE CHARGER OR SERVICE PLATE The charger is the decorative plate at each place setting. It can be silver, gold, embellished, floral, and so on. The charger is either removed in exchange for the entrée plate or the entrée is placed on top. It is not required but is purely a preference. The charger can be used instead of a placemat or just as a decorative element to set the mood.

SALAD PLATE The salad plate is placed to the left of the forks if preset.

BREAD PLATE WITH BUTTER KNIFE The bread plate goes above the forks, with the butter knife placed diagonally across the edge of the plate, handle on the right side and blade facing down.

DESSERT SPOON AND FORK These should be placed either horizontally above the dinner plate (the spoon on top with its handle facing to the right; the fork below with its handle facing left).

COFFEE CUP AND SAUCER The coffee cup and saucer are placed above and to the right of the knife and spoons. At home, most people serve coffee after the meal. In that case the cups and saucers are brought to the table and placed above and to the right of the knife and spoons.

the formal table

Never set a formal table with more than three knives and three forks. If you have more courses, bring the corresponding silverware out with that course.

Serving dishes should not be placed. Instead, they should be brought out with each course and offered to each guest. Condiments should be served, not placed (unless of course, the condiment dish is doubling as table décor).

BUFFET BEHAVIOR

Setting a buffet can be tricky, but there are certain guidelines to ensure your buffet is user friendly. For example, if you have a round table, don't put utensils in the middle, as guests could inadvertently dip their sleeve in the aioli. Plus, it may be confusing for them to figure out where to begin, which is why most buffets are console style. This is what we prefer and highly recommend.

1. Place plates at the beginning and silverware at the end, so guests have as little as possible in their hands when serving themselves. Place sauces next to the dish they accompany so no one confuses the balsamic vinegar with the soy sauce. Place bread at the far end of the buffet so guests can snag a piece at the end. That way it's not floating among the fare where it may get soggy.

2. Don't forget the utensils! Be sure to have a separate spoon, knife, fork, or whatever is required for each dish. Don't expect guests to use the same spatula for the herb-braised sea bass and the filet in a port wine reduction.

3. Be prepared for repeat visits. Chances are most of your guests will make more than one trip to the buffet, so stockpile enough silverware and dishes to accommodate them.

4. Provide ample space for people to sit and eat. And don't forget to include a place to rest their plates and cups.

5. Disposal is a big concern. Provide an obvious place for people to dispose of used dishes and utensils or hire a staff that will circulate through the room removing the dirty dishes.

6. Keep the guests informed of the food by having a server standing near the buffet station. They can help serve, inform guests of the ingredients, and keep the line moving. You can choose to place menu cards in front of each dish instead, but Lara prefers the personal touch.

Scenery Switcheroo

After serving dinner, consider moving to another room for dessert. Create a lounge-like environment, serve after-dinner cocktails, and light candles everywhere. Switching up the scene helps change the mood. If you want to rev up the evening, then make it more barlike. You can do this for any course. For example, Lara recently hosted a luncheon at the Hotel Bel-Air. The afternoon began with a short round of cocktails on the terrace (always keep afternoon cocktails short), then everyone moved inside for the luncheon. Afterward, a decadent dessert buffet was served in the garden. So chic, so cute. So ladies who lunch.

SAVVY SERVING

If you opt to serve your guests yourself, remember this cardinal rule: serve from the left, clear from the right. Wine is also poured and cleared from right. Other things to consider: if you are passing anything with handles, pass with the handle in the direction of the person receiving.

Also, be sure to make frequent passes through the room to pick up empty glasses, refill common bowls of munchies, and check on ice and other bar supplies.

chic tip

There's only one time paper plates are acceptable: a backyard barbecue. And even then, we are proponents of nicer serving options like acrylic dishes (Crate & Barrel has some great options), which not only look nicer, but are more eco-friendly. If you absolutely must go with the disposable dish, opt for the plastic dishware available at the grocery store. It's a dollar or two more, but it's certainly more elegant.

Stock up on Chinese-style takeout containers. If a guest compliments the food, package up some leftovers for them.

Table Talk

The host should always be aware of the dinner conversation. If there is a lull or if someone heads into dangerous territory, it is the host's duty to get things moving in the right direction. Try to draw everyone into a central conversation; fragmented side conversations and idle chit-chat can isolate other guests.

Suddenly silent? Don't panic. Chatter generally dies down for a bit when each course is served. It's just a lull and once everyone gets a forkful of food the conversation will naturally resume.

DIFFUSING DISASTERS

Even the most prepared host can run into one of many predicaments on party day. We've got the how-to on handling even the most vexing dilemma with ease.

p r o b l e m **The unexpected guest.** You've made it crystal clear that this is a dinner party for eight, but go figure, Lisa showed up with a guy she met last week.

s o l u t i o n **Be prepared.** It's inevitable. No matter how much you stress it's not okay to arrive with someone in tow, it continues to happen. Save yourself stress by anticipating such guest gaffes. Have extra chairs and place settings readily available just in case of unexpected additions. You should also keep extra pens and place cards on hand.

p r o b l e m **The solo guest.** You invited your Pilates' pal to a dinner party you are hosting for your office cohorts. She won't know anyone at the table. How do you avoid her having a long, lonely evening?

s o l u t i o n **You have two options.** One: seat the solo surfer next to or as close to you as possible. That way she feels like she belongs and you can lead the introductions. Two: seat her next to someone you know she will like. Maybe one of your co-workers is a Pilates nut or has been dying to try it out, and this means the two have some common ground. Be preemptive and tell both parties ahead of time about your seating strategy.

problem **Catfight!** Love them dearly, but Jennifer and Ashley can't stand to be in the same room with each other. Unfortunately, they are two of your closest friends and you definitely want them at your engagement dinner!

solution **A catfight or bitchy one-liners will make everyone feel awkward.** However, if the overlap is inevitable, sidestep a hair-pulling catastrophe using strategy. This means keeping the adversaries as far apart as possible, at different tables, preferably across the room! If you're planning on one long table, position the enemies on the same side of the table so they are less likely to be in the other's line of vision. Out of sight, out of mind!

problem **Remember Lisa and her uninvited date?** He's sitting at the table waiting expectantly for dinner to arrive.

solution **Extra, extra!** Always prepare extra food. But if you do end up with a superfluous guest and you have only prepared fourteen servings of each item, you will have to improvise. Don't forfeit your own dish; it will only make your guest feel more awkward. Instead, split the offender's dish in two and divide between two plates.

problem **The late arrival.** Two of your guests are late for your dinner party that was scheduled to begin at 8:30 on the dot. What now?

solution **Dinner parties are not meant to be fluid,** so guests should arrive on time. In general, you do not have to wait for a latecomer, especially if you have already allotted a grace period in the form of pre-dinner drinks. Start the meal promptly as planned and when the stragglers arrive, get them situated at the table and serve them the course that the rest of the guests are eating. For smaller parties, a host may choose to wait for guests who have called ahead. Even so, for the sake of the other guests who did show up on time, don't wait more than fifteen minutes.

problem **You've carefully planned your menu,** finished the grocery shopping, and now at the last minute you discover one of your guests has a dietary restriction.

solution **If someone keeps kosher, or is vegetarian,** or has any kind of dietary restrictions, usually they will tell you in advance. That way you can have an appropriate dish prepared. But sometimes you don't get the memo for one reason or another; perhaps the person didn't want to bother you or is just straight up inconsiderate. The best plan is to always have something around that's healthy, like salad or green veggies.

for the guest

Today, there are far more important things for a guest to worry about than keeping their elbows off the table. Not chewing with your mouth open or talking with your mouth full just scratches the surface of the table decree (although those statutes certainly do still apply).

place card protocol

If you are at a party that has place cards, never move them. As we mentioned, seating is calculated/strategic and it is never your prerogative to shift it to suit your wishes. There are so many girls in the New York social scene who are known for this move. If you know a place card offender is in your midst, just keep an eye on them and if need be, ask them to keep the cards as is.

napkin etiquette

- Napkin etiquette is simple. Put the napkin in your lap and leave it there until the meal is over. We say lap and we mean it. Don't tuck it in your collar or anything like that. If you get up during the meal, place your napkin either on the chair or just to the left of your place setting. The latter has the added bonus of avoiding the transfer of anything from the napkin to the seat of your very posh denim.

- When you return, put the napkin back on your lap. Never place your napkin back on the table until the meal is over. Period.

- Wipe your mouth before swigging your Merlot. Truly, it is always unpleasant to leave lipstick kisses on the rim of your glass.

- While we admire your wanting to help, for heaven's sake, do not dive under the table to chase your napkin or anything that may have found its way off the table.

buffet behavior

When you are at a party where the fare is self-serve remember these guidelines.

- Don't take your dirty plate back for round two. If you opt for seconds, place your dirty dish wherever it is being collected, or throw it away if it's disposable.

- Always use the serving utensils provided, and do not even think about using your hands for anything that is not clearly finger food.

- Don't pick at your plate as you are loading up. Eating off your plate while waiting in line can be distracting or disgusting to fellow guests.

- Don't pile your plate high. The beauty of a buffet is that seconds (or thirds) is always an option.

picky palate

There will be times when you are faced with food that you don't like or don't want. If you have specific dietary restrictions, make it easier on everyone and alert your host ahead of time. Simply lay out your culinary confines when you RSVP. If you simply don't like the food, that is another story. Do you refuse? You can always decline passed food, but do not refuse placed food. Let the server put it in front of you, fake a bite or two of whatever you can stand, and hold tight for the next course. What if you take a bite and don't like it? Choke it down! If you must spit it out (really, can't you try to swallow it!), do so into your napkin. Fake a cough, or *something*.

eating etiquette

- There are times when it's okay to eat with your hands; sometimes it is even preferable. There is something a bit awkward about eating certain foods, say cherry tomatoes, with a knife and fork. Determining when it's okay, however, can be tricky. Generally, you can be sure that formal occasions mean your digits aren't acceptable utensils. However, there is such a thing as finger food: pizza, corn on the cob, fried chicken, French fries, tacos, and such. If you're in doubt, follow the lead of the host. If they are using a fork, you should as well.

- Community munching is always tricky. Do avoid double dipping at all costs. There are two options: dip deep, or break off small pieces of whatever you're dipping.

- Don't ever put food that you've touched back on a common tray.

- Is it okay to eat the last piece? Absolutely! If you simply cannot get enough of the tapas, feel free to take it down. Just ask if anyone else wants it first.

- Tasting off another's plate: we are not the biggest fan of this practice but if you simply must sample your tablemate's soufflé, do not reach across the table—you might knock over your neighbor's Pinot Noir. Instead, have them put a bite-size portion on your plate or bread plate and pass it to you.

when to start eating

Determining when to dig in can be tricky. There are some telltale signs to watch for—it's usually when everyone has their food and the host will ask people to begin. Or there may be a toast, or a simple "bon appétit" will be the signal to dive in.

In general, look to your host for your cue; when they start eating, the rest of the table is free to follow. Of course, if it's a buffet you can start chowing down once the buffet line has been opened.

Bottom line, keep this rule in the back of your mind: You should never be the only one eating. Still confused? Here are a few event-specific situations.

IN-HOME SOIREE Wait until the host takes the first bite before you begin to eat. If your host is engaged in conversation, look to other guests for your cue. If everyone else is eating, feel free to dive in. At more casual events, if the table is waiting to follow the host's lead, you can crack a joke: "We're starving here!"

BUFFET Self-serve can be tricky. If you have piled your plate high but are the first to sit at the table, wait a moment until the table fills up to dig in. If after five minutes your tablemates are still posted at the buffet, go ahead and enjoy your fare solo.

RESTAURANT If others are served first, or vice versa, wait until everyone is served to begin eating. It is terribly tacky to dive into your tuna tartare prematurely.

NO TABLE, NO WAITING! In self-serve situations, especially those where you are eating standing up, consume as you please.

TABLE TURF

Navigating the turf of the table is always tricky. But nothing takes the enjoyment out of a meal more than wondering, "Did he just drink my water??" Avoid turf wars by considering this simple tip: liquids are on the right, solids on the left. Still confused? One way to remember this set up: BMW—no, not the "7-series" you've been obsessing over, but *bread, meal, water* (from left to right). So pause to remember this before lunging at that sourdough roll.

We have all sat down to a meal at some point in our life only to be completely overwhelmed by the amount of silver and glass on the table. For a formal place setting you should have exactly as much silverware as you will need, arranged in precisely the right order.

The key is to begin with the silverware on the outside of the place setting and work your way in with each course. When in doubt, watch the host and follow suit!

For a midmeal pause, place your utensils on your plate. When you're finished with your meal, the host or waiter will likely swoop in momentarily to clear your place. In the meantime, place your utensils on your plate. The utensils should be parallel and diagonal

(4 o'clock) with knife blade facing the center of the plate. Whatever you do, do not place used utensils back on the table (and yes, this counts even if the tablecloth is red-and-white-checked).

There's a reason people buy extra place settings and additional glassware: accidents. Things break, extra people show up unannounced, and you need to be prepared. If you think you need place settings for eight, buy for ten. That way if something breaks or an extra guest arrives, you're covered!

CODE OF CONDUCT

However adept you may be at distinguishing cutlery, you must also be proficient at conducting yourself properly at the table.

TABLE TALK No matter how proficient you are at wielding eating utensils, you must also be able to hold proper table conversation. Don't scream across the table. If you are dying to dish on your current crush, wait until after the meal. At a seated meal, pay equal attention to your dining companions on either side of you.

If you make a gaffe at the table, you need to be prepared to recover gracefully. The main goal is to avoid distracting other guests or drawing attention to yourself. If your slip is subtle, meaning your fumble didn't upset another guest (or ruin their clothing, or the host's tablecloth, rug, or couch), then simply continue without further ado.

ELECTRONIC ETIQUETTE There are certain things that simply have no place at the table, like your BlackBerry, cell phone, or any other device of that nature. However, if you simply cannot bear the thought of parting with your PDA, make sure it is on silent or vibrate. If you absolutely must make a call or write an urgent e-mail, excuse yourself! Never, ever do it at the table. And under no circumstances is it okay to place any of your devices on the table. Last, when you are at any party, no matter how casual or formal, your phone should always be on silent or vibrate.

While we can't stress enough the importance of leaving your BlackBerry, Sidekick, Treo, iPhone, and so on in your purse or pocket, there are times when they are a necessity. For example, Lara often sends herself a reminder when she and a guest discuss something that will need followup. If you have to do this, make a joke about how forgetful you are and then put the gadget away. Don't use necessity as an excuse to check e-mails or listen to voice mail! However, if it's a formal dinner party, taking out gadgets is an absolute no-no. Such behavior is only okay at a casual gatherings.

TRADING NUMBERS There is only one time when it's okay to take out your BlackBerry—to get telephone numbers. The days of scratching them down on paper are over, so people tend to pull out their PDAs to exchange phone numbers or e-mail addresses.

Tasteless or Tolerable

DO   Engage in conversation with your tablemates—as many as possible

          Compliment the food (especially if it's homemade)

          Excuse yourself if you have something in your teeth. Picking in public is not an option.

          Pace yourself. Don't eat too fast or too slow. Stay in line with your dining companions to maintain the tempo of the meal.

          Keep all personal belongings off the table

          Always inform tablemates or dining partners if they have something in their teeth or on their face

DON'T   Crunch on ice cubes

          Blow your nose, especially into the napkin. A napkin should never double as a tissue!

          Engage in excessive primping at the table (ideally none at all). If it is dire that you reapply, excuse yourself and go to the restroom.

          Push your plate away when you are finished

          Season or salt before tasting. Your assumption of blandness could be offensive to the chef.

          Answer your phone. In fact, don't even look at your BlackBerry, Sidekick, caller ID, or have any sort of electronic interlude during dinner or even more important, in the middle of a conversation.

seven

COCKTAIL CONDUCT

how to hold your liquor, my friend

GREAT LIBATIONS are one of the most important elements of any party. But the etiquette of serving cocktails comes with responsibility. Not only do you need to think about how to serve the beverages (drink cart, bartender, iced down in buckets), but a host must provide a wide selection, pay attention to the proportions, and most important, be careful not to overserve. Getting your guests sloshed is not the mark of a good host. Doing that, my friends, is for an all-night college party. Simply put, there are five basic elements to consider when planning a drink menu for any event, whether it's at 9 a.m. or 9 p.m.

1. Always serve beverages.

2. Be certain to have enough glasses and ice.

3. Select a wide assortment of drinks.

4. Offer nonalcoholic beverages.

5. Do not, under any circumstances, allow anyone to drink and drive.

Design a drink menu well in advance. Consider what types of beverages you want to serve and whether or not you want to establish or carry through a theme. For a holiday like the Fourth of July, you might want to serve red, white, and blue drinks or for Halloween, a martini garnished with a miniature black cat. Planning your menu will allow you to add these kinds of unique touches. For example, Lara loves to make bright-colored cocktails and line the tray with candy.

When creating a drink menu, it's not only acceptable but also expected that a host will serve drinks that coordinate with the theme of their party, and in some cases, with their home furnishings. By this, we mean that if your house is a study in white, beige, cream, or any stainable color, it's perfectly fine to limit the drinks to clear liquids. Just find a wide range of choices, such as Champagne, white wine, sparkling apple juice, white grape juice, vodka, gin, and rum. Be clever with your mixers to make the drinks fun—for example, white grape juice martinis.

take note   It is always good to offer coffee, including decaf. But in doing so, make sure you have all of the appropriate accoutrements. You should have milk, half-and-half, cream, sugar, and sugar substitutes like Equal or Splenda. It's also nice to offer a selection of teas, including green and herbal, with and without caffeine.

for the host

Cocktails are a mainstay of most parties and it is the hosts' job to provide guests with a bevy of beverages. And please, refrain from going the BYOB (Bring Your Own Booze) route. The only time we find this to be a wise move is when the event calls for guest-provided alcohol, say at a wine-tasting party.

Here are some points to consider when crafting your drink menu.

THIRST QUENCHERS

Create a signature cocktail. At Harrison & Shriftman events we are known for designing new drinks. Lara and Elizabeth adore creating custom cocktails. Often when coming up with a new drink, they look to some of their favorites, which include the mojito, the Ivy Gimlet, the Palms' S'mores, and Nobu's Passionfruit Sake, and then give them a new twist. Just make sure the new concoction tastes as good as it looks. Another method is to simply rename a classic drink to make it your own. So if it's a Valentine Dinner for couples serve a Cosmopolitan, but call it a Love Potion, or make rum 'n' Coke but call it a One Night Stand. Just have fun with it!

Remember to offer nonalcoholic options! Soft drinks, sparkling cider, lemonade, flavored waters, IZZE drinks, root beer . . . the list goes on forever. Pay just as much attention to how you serve the nonalcoholic beverages as you do the liquor. Pour lemonade in a wine goblet and garnish with a wedge of lemon, lime, or a fresh raspberry, add a green apple wedge to sparkling cider, and so on.

Offer guests a drink as soon as they arrive. At Harrison & Shriftman events, we always station servers at the door to greet guests with a tray of drinks upon arrival. Make sure that there are at least a couple of options offered on the tray, perhaps your signature cocktail and some bubbly. Then guests will feel free to mingle instead of dashing off to the bar.

SAVVY SERVING

if you choose to hire servers

Make sure the servers are up to speed. If you have a specialty cocktail, brief the servers on the recipe. Guests will always ask, "What's in it?" Or better yet, make a cute menu for the bar so guests know what is being served.

do it yourself

If instead of hiring a bartender, you opt to serve guests yourself, whether by setting up a self-serve bar or setting up bottle service stations throughout the party space, remember that self-serve does not mean fend for yourself. Make sure that you provide guests with ample options. Consider choosing a couple of different brands of vodka and gin, or if you're going with a Mexican theme, options of tequila and beer. That way everyone can find something that suits their taste buds.

If you are taking on bartending duties and aren't comfortable with stirring, shaking, and blending, then get a lesson! Whether you log on to Wikipedia, purchase a bartending guide at the bookstore, or get lessons from a friend, it's all about practice. Our best tip is to go to a local restaurant or bar on an off time and get the bartender to teach you how to make a few standard and specialty drinks. Remember, practice makes perfect!

And if you don't know how to make the drink order? Don't fret, simply inform the guest you're not familiar with the mixers and ask how to make it. If you're still unsure, ask for a demonstration and have fun with the situation. And guests, please, try not to be picky with your order. Before calling out a complicated request, look around the bar and see what is on hand and order accordingly.

Vodka is always a safe bet because it provides a variety of options: it mixes with any kind of juice, soda, or tonic, and it can be served on the rocks or straight up. At a loss when it comes to stocking the bar? Follow our bartending guide:

- 1 to 3 bottles of vodka

- 1 bottle of gin

- 1 bottle of tequila

- 1 bottle of rum

- 1 bottle of whiskey

- Beer, red and white wine, and Champagne. Having all four on hand is best, but not a must. And if you're strapped for funds, it's okay to have only enough Champagne for one glass per guest for a group toast.

- Be sure you have a variety of mixers, plenty of ice, and the basic garnishes (lemons and limes). Remember to monitor mixers, ice, and garnishes throughout the night and refill as needed.

No matter how you choose to serve, the most important thing to remember is to be well stocked. Nothing dampens the mood like running dry midway through your soiree. Bank on each guest consuming three cocktails. If you're expecting twenty people, you'll need sixty glasses of wine, or ten bottles (a standard wine bottle pours about six glasses). A 750-milliliter bottle of vodka yields thirteen two-ounce martinis. A nine-bottle bar should meet all your cocktail needs. Add a few extra bottles for safety—a cushion is always recommended.

Choosing the brand of liquor can be a difficult decision. People have favorites, and some people will only drink a certain brand; they have to have their Grey Goose or Johnny Walker, so consider keeping a couple of different brands of the big three on hand, gin, vodka and Scotch.

If you do run out, act quickly (and suavely). Call a local grocer who delivers or, if there isn't one in your area, ask one of your servers or your co-host to hit the road, stat!

bubblin' up

Champagne can be a budget breaker and as such, it's not a requirement for celebrations. If you want something fizzy without the price tag, look for Italian proseccos or a sparkling white wine from California. If you really want to pop the cork, serve each person one glass at the appropriate time—the cutting of the birthday cake, at the beginning of the meal, or when it comes time for a big toast. On the other hand, there are times when Champagne can be the only drink, namely at a brunch or luncheon. Offer selections by creating mimosas, bellinis, kir royals, and so on.

The popping of the cork is the international signal for celebration. But aim that cork in the wrong direction or tug it off improperly and you'll have a mass of bubbles tumbling all over the place—plus you might take out an eye! We asked the fine crafters of Veuve Clicquot Champagne to tell us the proper way of uncorking the bubbly.

COOLING

- Place the bottle in a bucket filled with ice and water.
- Leave the bottle to chill for twenty minutes, when it will be at the right temperature of 46 to 50 degrees F.

OPENING THE BOTTLE

- Remove the foil by unwinding it counterclockwise around the bottle.
- Place thumb on top of cork.
- Untwist the wire, keeping thumb on top of cork to ensure cork will not pop.
- Place other hand on the bottom of the bottle.
- Wrap hand around cork, twisting and pulling simultaneously until cork pops.

TASTING When tasting champagne, all five senses are used.

1. EARS Listen to the pop of the cork. Look at it as an invitation into the bottle. Listen to the bubbles as they dance inside the glass.

2. EYES Enjoy the gold reflections of the Champagne.

3. NOSE Smell the rich scent of fruit and flowers.

4. TASTE Take a small sip and confirm the scent by tasting the Champagne's fruity character.

5. TOUCH Feel the bubbles on your palate and detect both the bready and buttery taste.

STORING Store the bottle in a place that has a consistent temperature of 50 to 55 degrees F. The storage area should have a high level of humidity in the region of 80 percent, and very good ventilation with no lights whatsoever.

chic tip   Short lived! Before you rummage out the dusty Moët that you got for Christmas last year, remember that Champagne and sparkling whites have a shelf life of only six months to a year.

GET TO KNOW YOUR GLASSWARE

If, by chance, you end up behind the bar playing bartender, there are certain things you need to know—like a tumbler from a highball. This is especially noteworthy when tackling wine. Grape connoisseurs take the shape and size of their glasses seriously and pairing the right wine with the correct glass is essential for the enjoyment of wine. Study these basics and then feel free to dress them up with glassware that is etched, painted, or tinted—though keep in mind that oenophiles prefer their glasses clear so they can fully appreciate the color and clarity of the wine.

COLLINS With a shape similar to a highball glass, but taller, this standard was originally used for Collins gin drinks. Today it's the serving choice for soft drinks and tropical-inspired drinks such as mai tais. Typically 14 ounces.

CORDIAL Small, stemmed glass used to serve liqueurs at the end of a meal. Typically 1 to 2 ounces.

OLD-FASHIONED Short, round glass suitable for cocktails or liquor served on the rocks or "with a splash" (whiskey with a splash of water). Typically holds between 9 and 12 ounces.

HIGHBALL This straight-sided glass is an elegant way to serve mixed drinks, such cranberry and vodka, gin and tonic, or any drink on the rocks. Typically holds 8 to 12 ounces.

Signature cocktails from the Palms Casino Resort at the Fergie concert after-party

SHOT Perfect for pouring a one-ounce shot of vodka, whiskey, or any other liquor. Necessary for mixing drinks. Typically, they are 1¼ ounces, with a line denoting the one-ounce measurement.

WHITE WINE The bowl should be medium-size and taper inward at the top, as this shape allows the wine's aroma to fill the nose. Typically between 8 and 14 ounces.

RED WINE Red wine glasses have a larger, rounder bowl than a white wine glass and a slight taper at the top of the bowl. Typically between 10 and 16 ounces.

CHAMPAGNE AND SPARKLING WHITES These tall, tapered flutes are designed to keep the bubbles active. Typically 5 ounces.

BEER There are a variety of glasses from Pilsner to steins, but as a rule of thumb, the best glass to go with is the pint glass, as it is sturdy and works well with a variety of cold brews.

take note Don't fill it to the rim! Just because that red wine glass holds 16 ounces doesn't mean you need to pour 16 ounces. Aim to fill the glass to about one-third of its capacity. Not only is this proper, but it deters spills! Always hold wine glasses by the stem, as the hand may heat up the wine and change the flavor. Of course, this is unavoidable if you're going stemless!

chic tip

Wondering what to do with all that leftover liquor? We asked Allison Sarofim, a contributing editor of *Domino* magazine, how she deals with excess. "Keep the liquor or return the unused bottles to the liquor store for credit."

WINE 101

Wine is a staple at parties. While we are not implying that you need to be a connoisseur, being fluent in at least the fundamentals of wine is always encouraged.

You do not have to be an expert to serve wine with ease. This basic know-how will allow you to wine and dine your guests effortlessly. Consider these tips when crafting your menu. Generally speaking, red wine is paired with red meats and pastas with tomato sauces. White wines are generally paired with fish, chicken, salads, and pasta dishes with light sauces.

Pairing Chart

Here are some perfect pairings.

Italian dinner **Sauvignon Blanc**

Backyard barbecue (burgers) **Cabernet Sauvignon**

Barbecued seafood **Riesling**

Salad supper **Pinot Noir**

Hamptons-style clambake **Chardonnay**

If you are tapping into your existing stash, be wary of choosing a bottle that is past its prime. However, don't fret if you find an overly aged bottle. Put it aside and use it for cooking for up to a month or freeze it for the marinade at your next dinner party.

Take care not to overchill your vino. Pop your bottle in the fridge an hour before you plan to serve. White wine is best served at 55 degrees, red at room temperature. If you opt to leave an open bottle at the table for easy access, white wines should always be kept in a cooler; red may be left on the table or chilled.

Use glass markers so guests don't get their glasses confused. Don't risk a guest taking a swig from someone else's Merlot.

If you are entertaining in a restaurant and footing the bill make sure that you choose a few bottles of wine beforehand. Giving guests free rein with the wine list could leave you with a hefty tab.

proper pouring

When pouring wine, turn the bottle ever so slightly when you are finished pouring to avoid dripping. A wine glass should be only a quarter to a third full.

Once you decide what will go in your glass, you must know how to hold it. If you are drinking red wine, hold the glass by the bowl. If you are drinking white, hold by the stem so as not to warm the drink.

Decanter and goblets from Lara Shriftman and Elizabeth Harrison's line, Party Confidential, for Home Shopping Network

Photo credit: John Shearer/WireImage

TRICKY TERMS

APERITIFS "Openers," the precursors to a meal meant to prep taste buds for flavors to come. Traditional choices include Pernod or Lillet, but Champagne or rosé served before the food can suffice. Small, not meant to be full drinks.

BOTTLE SERVICE A setup of glasses, booze on ice, and a variety of mixers—typically cranberry juice, orange juice, seltzer, and tonic. At a nightclub, the price of bottle service includes a dedicated server, which is one of the reasons that ordinary bottle of Grey Goose suddenly costs $300.

Choosing Wine at a Restaurant

1. Choose a bottle from the menu.

2. The server will show you the label of the bottle.

3. The server will uncork the bottle and present the cork to you.

4. The server will pour a sip into your glass for you to taste.

5. Swirl/smell.

6. A nod of approval will do.

7. Other guests at the table should have their glasses filled after you taste.

CORDIALS Sweet-flavored liqueurs, the perfect complement to the end of a meal.

DIGESTIVES/AFTER-DINNER DRINKS Cognacs, ports, late-harvest wines. Their full-bodied essence is said to settle the stomach.

If you want to bring your own wine to the restaurant, it's completely fine if the restaurant allows. Most establishments will charge you a corkage fee ranging from $10 to $35. Check beforehand because some places won't let you bring in wine, and you can negotiate this beforehand. People may bring wine to save money, but often it's a special bottle of wine they have picked out for the occasion.

GRACIOUS GUEST

There are certain codes that dictate table time. At a dinner party, if you are holding a half-consumed cocktail when asked to sit down, it is perfectly kosher to take it with you to the table. If you do not want a drink at the table do not flip your glass over. When the server offers, simply place your hand over the glass and decline gracefully. A simple "no, thank you" will always suffice.

And keep in mind that at a restaurant, don't order the most expensive bottle of wine or drink—leave the Macallen 30 for another time when you're footing the bill, or you will wear out your welcome. Taking a cue from the host is the best way to handle top shelf anxiety. If she orders the standard house pour, follow her lead.

NIGHT OWLS

Confused about the laws of the nightclub? Don't get left standing on the wrong side of the velvet rope. Experts Andrew Goldberg, the director of VIP services for Marquee NYC and Tao Las Vegas, and Rich Thomas, the marketing director and door manager at Marquee NYC, spell out the decorum for a night out on the town. Read, learn, memorize from the masters!

how do you make a reservation for a table?

ANDREW GOLDBERG "Try to get in contact with the lead table host! Besides the owners, this individual has the largest inventory of tables in the nightclub."

RICH THOMAS "The best way to make a reservation is to call ahead of time and be totally clear about the number in your party and the male/female ratio. I would also advise those who are not club savvy to make sure that men wear button-down shirts with a blazer. Looking your best can never hurt."

explain the phenomenon of bottle service.

ANDREW GOLDBERG "Bottle service is for someone who values the comfort of sitting rather than standing at the bar. It is for someone who's willing to pay a premium for prime real estate in a nightclub, and most of all, it is for someone who wants to rub elbows with the in crowd or at least try to emulate them for one night!"

what do you do if someone reserves a table and some-one else sits there?

ANDREW GOLDBERG "It is imperative that all customers know that if they buy drinks at the bar and then proceed to sit at a bottle service table they will have to move by midnight. The phrase our staff utilizes reads like this: 'All tables are reserved for bottle customers and if you would like a table I will get a bottle host for your convenience. All of our waitresses and security guards have been briefed on this procedure.' It is a critical service point because bar patrons are still 40 percent of our business and we can't alienate such a large percentage of our revenue."

what do you do when someone else sits at your reserved table and orders drinks on your tab?

RICH THOMAS "The person who has the credit card down should always let the server know exactly who at the table is allowed to order. This will prevent crashers from ordering on the principal's tab."

how much do you usually tip on one drink?

ANDREW GOLDBERG "If the drink is $7.55 always leave the change and add a dollar on top of it. This only goes for drinks under $10."

RICH THOMAS "Most people leave at least one or two dollars' tip per drink."

what if someone forgets to tip?

ANDREW GOLDBERG "We add 20 percent service charge to all bottle service checks to help alleviate this problem."

RICH THOMAS "If someone orders a drink at the bar and does not leave a tip, nothing can be done about that."

do you tip per drink or at the end of the night?

ANDREW GOLDBERG "You tip large when you order the first round so the bartender will give you preferential treatment throughout the night. A bartender always remembers a generous patron."

RICH THOMAS "It is always best to tip per drink so that the bartender knows he is being taken care of. I'm sure a situation has happened to a bartender where he thought a nice tip was coming at the end of the night and he was stiffed, so if he sees the tips coming throughout the night that is one less worry."

what do you do if someone wants to come to a party and you don't want them to come?

ANDREW GOLDBERG "Let them know it is a private party for a client and they have full control of the guest list for the evening. Always be stoic and apologize and invite them to come back for another evening."

how do you ask someone to leave a party or a club?

ANDREW GOLDBERG "That's the toughest part of night life, and it takes a customer service specialist. This individual must have immense patience and thick skin because he will be bruising the ego of a person who is most likely intoxicated and ready for a verbal dispute. To combat their inability to rationalize the situation you must be prepared to have educated answers on why the guest is being asked to leave. That means you must meet with all parties involved before you make the ejection. Let the guest say their piece, and never, and I repeat never, interrupt them because it will incite them even more. When they are finished explain why you came to this decision and stay calm and firm and nine out of ten times they respect the outcome."

RICH THOMAS "You have security do it. This way you are not looked at as the 'bad guy.'"

how do you tell people "no" about bringing too many guests?

ANDREW GOLDBERG "You quietly whisper in their ear that I just had to deny my own cousin because he had too large a party! People tend not to argue when family is involved."

RICH THOMAS "Kindly tell them that capacity is limited, so you had to set a general rule that no extra guests are allowed."

DIFFUSING DISASTER

Drinks often invite problems, disorderly guests, questions about drinking habits, and more. Here are our solutions to those soggy situations.

problem **You just ordered a bottle of wine only to discover that your date is going with a Diet Coke.** How do you handle the situation when you are drinking and the other is not?

solution **Never pressure nondrinkers** or ask why they are not drinking. If they don't want to tell you, that's their business. There's no reason to even acknowledge or comment on their choice to abstain. It's incredibly inappropriate to question why someone is not drinking, not to mention invasive. They may offer up a reason, which could be as simple as: I just don't feel like having anything to drink, I'm on a diet (red wine is all carbs!), my head is killing me, I'm an alcoholic, or anything. The reason need not be expanded on unless the person invites further conversation.

If you are on the receiving end and don't want to expand on your reasons for not drinking, simply repeat what you ordered and respond, "I am drinking, I ordered the Diet Coke," or simply, "I just don't want to."

problem **Someone has just sent you a free round of drinks.** Do you have to reciprocate?

solution **If you'd like to do so, then do it!** Whatever you decide, be sure to acknowledge the offer by raising your glass in a toast in the direction of the sender before taking the first sip. Don't forget to send a thank-you via the server who presented the free round. If you don't want the drink, be gracious nonetheless, just take a sip or simply hold the glass up as a toast and set it back down.

problem **The drunk guest.** After spending the night propped against the bar and draining Champagne like water, Slurry Shawn is raucously lurching around, bumping into guests, leering at the ladies, and you're sure he's going to spew more than just words onto your carpet.

s o l u t i o n   **Hail to the cab!** This is where your co-host can help out, since she can keep the guests entertained while you get Mr. Slurry under control (or vice versa). Always have a taxi number on hand. It goes without saying, but don't ever let a guest drive while intoxicated. If you expect a bash has gone wild inform guests that you've called a fleet of taxis to take everyone home and that they can retrieve their cars in the morning.

* Politely ask Mr. Slurry to stop drinking and offer a nonalcoholic beverage like a bottle of water or cup of coffee (though the latter won't actually do anything to sober him up, it does help change the mood from party party to slow down).

* Give 'em carbs! Have your co-host make a McDonald's run or order pizza and get all that alcohol soaked up and Mr. Slurry will settle down.

* Drink removal! Ask the bartender to stop serving an intoxicated guest. If Mr. Slurry becomes offended or angry, you or your co-host should immediately step in and explain that he's had enough to drink.

* G'night, Mr. Slurry. If the above approaches don't work, then it's time to tuck him in bed. Call a taxi or ask a friend to escort him outta there. Bottom line, send him on his way home, ASAP! If he's already nodding off and you're comfortable with a house guest, then schlep him into your guest bedroom (not the one with everyone's coats and purses) and close the door. Tightly.

problem **The waiter has been filling up your glass all night long,** and now you're more than a bit tipsy—with a spanking huge bill to boot!

solution **Suck it up and deal!** Not only is this standard, good service, but it's up to you to monitor your drinking. In the future, politely ask the server to refrain from refilling your glass. Keep in mind that true professionals are trained to elusively fill your glass; you have to pay attention if you don't want to continue consuming alcohol.

Don't Be the Drunk Girl

Nightmares happen to every host! Recently Lara hosted a dinner party for one of her clients only to have the publicist for the company become incredibly intoxicated—we'll say it, *hammered.* Guests at the party nicknamed the flack "Drunk Girl" as they watched her aggressively hitting on the men present, invading everyone's space, slurring her words, boobs falling out of her dress, and just straight up acting like a drunken ass. In fact, guests became so annoyed by the drunken display that they began leaving! To make matters worse, upon being asked to leave, she requested a "roadie" (a drink for the road). Needless to say, one wasn't provided.

CELEBRITIES ON COCKTAILS

Celebrities attend hundreds of parties a year and needless to say are well versed in the cocktail code of conduct. We asked some of our closest celeb pals, "What is your favorite drink at a party?"

"Martinis."   Nicky Hilton

"Mixed martinis, margaritas, and mojitos."   Molly Sims

"Champagne with fresh apple juice."   Venus Williams

"I like to spike punch."   David Arquette

"Ketel One on the rocks."   Michael Kors

"Patron on the rocks, with lime."   Bijou Phillips

"I like to drink cranberry with lime juice and sparkling water. That's what I drink when I am not in the mood to have alcohol. Or a good glass of wine. I like Bâtard-Montrachet."

                                                      Forest Whitaker

"Strawberry margaritas with Patrón or Corzo."   Stephen Dorff

"Any cocktail served at Ian Schrager's Gramercy Park Hotel."
                                                      Michael Michele

eight

GET TOASTED

here's looking at you, kid!

A FABULOUS TOAST can turn an ordinary occasion into an extraordinary celebration and make a simple moment special. On the other hand, a terrible toast can quickly dampen even the fiercest soiree. This chapter will arm you with everything you need to know, no matter which side of the toast you are on. *Salute!*

TOP FIVE TOASTING TIPS

No matter the occasion, there are some fundamentals to consider before raising your glass. While some of the best toasts are impromptu, remember there is a protocol. Toasting protocol depends on the situation. For example, a simple "cheers" will do when dining with a small group of friends, whereas at a large benefit, gala, or wedding a prepared speech should always be in hand. Here are our no-fail tips for making a fabulous toast.

1. Generally speaking, the host should offer the first toast. If you are not the host, wait until the host raises a glass before piping up. However, at less formal events or casual get-togethers where there isn't an official guest of honor, it is okay for a guest to propose a toast, usually to honor or thank the host. Either way, whoever initiates should always make sure everyone's glasses are full!

2. Cheers! Sipping your drink at the conclusion of the toast seals the deal. Let us reiterate, we say "sip" for a reason. Chugging or guzzling is reserved for frat brother reunions.

3. Don't toast with an empty glass. More important, never refuse to participate in a toast. It's more polite to participate with a nonalcoholic beverage than not at all. Just don't fill 'er with water! Toasting with water is considered bad luck, so pour in something sparkling, whether it's Champagne or cider.

4. It is okay to honor more than one person per toast, especially if there are multiple hosts or special guests. Just be sure to keep each toast shorter than the previous one. No one wants to sit through an endless barrage!

5. Window to the soul. Yep, we're talking about eye contact. Always, always look the person you are toasting directly in the eyes. Not only does it make the toast more personal, but they know it's all about them!

FLAWLESS DELIVERY

Do not clink your glass. If you are delivering the toast, then stand up. Okay, you don't have to when you're out sharing cocktails with three gal pals. But in the cases of four or more, it's safe to say standing is required. Everyone else, including the person being toasted, remains seated. Raise your glass, clear your throat, and ask for everyone's attention. Don't leave your arm in the air during your toast. Lower your glass while saying your piece and then when you're finished speaking, raise your glass to signal the end.

SUBJECT MATTERS

Writing a toast can be intimidating, so instead of curling into the fetal position, refer to these ten fail-safe instructions when drafting your ode.

1. The most important thing to remember when writing a toast is to make it short, sweet, and snappy. We suggest keeping toasts to no more than one minute—at the most. Nothing ruins a party faster than a prolonged three-page acceptance speech-cum-toast. Besides, some of the best toasts are just a single line or two. Bottom line: whatever you say, get to the point!

2. The toast should spotlight the honoree—not the speaker.

3. Match the toast to both the honoree's personality and the event.

4. Choose simple but substantial words. A toast is not a forum to showcase your vast vocabulary. Often the simplest words sound the most sincere.

5. Make a fabulous statement by using a tried and true toast, part of a famous quote, poem, or speech, or even a line from a movie that sums up the moment.

6. The content of your toast is extremely important. Even a seamless delivery can be tainted by inappropriate material. The best toasts employ a good balance of humor, interest, and meaning.

7. Lighten up! There is no need to be overly eloquent; instead, think witty and charming. Make a joke or think of something funny to say (if it's occasion-appropriate). A little humor can salvage even the stuffiest of toasts. That being said there is a huge difference between funny and just plain vulgar. Weave some amusing anecdotes into your toast, but please, refrain from saying anything that will embarrass the honoree; it is not a roast!

8. If the assembled group is close, then refer to shared experiences, but don't make the toast a private joke between you and a select few.

9. Do mention and reflect on any outstanding accomplishments or unusually brave, heroic, romantic, or otherwise awesome acts performed by the toastee, especially if that's the reason for this grandiose gala!

10. Don't give a toast when you've had one too many. Slurring out a senseless speech doesn't honor anyone.

chic tip   Tailor your toast to your beverage or theme by using an authentic toast. For example, if you serve up sake at your next Asian-themed soiree impress your guests with a bona fide Japanese toast like "Kanpai!" (Cheers!)

CHEERS DEARS

Scripting your toast is only half of the battle. This is a time when those college classes on public speaking will come in handy. So if the thought of speaking in front of a crowd makes you want to run and hide, consider handing over the duties to someone who is unfazed by the situation. Stellar delivery and a charismatic speaker will captivate the crowd no matter what words are being said!

- Never push someone to make a toast. The crowd will end up shifting uncomfortably in their seats and counting the moments to the clink-clink of the Champagne glasses. You may end up hearing a toast you would just as soon wish you never had.

- If you give a toast after someone else, strive to make it creative and different. Duplicate dialogue is a waste of everyone's time. Make your toast more succinct than the last. In general, subsequent toasts should decrease in length as they go on.

- Do not inundate the crowd with toast after toast. If several people beat you to it, let the moment pass.

- Few things can ruin a special moment more than an inappropriate ode by a tipsy toaster. There is nothing worse than a guest who is three drinks deep deciding to raise their glass. A host must intervene, nip it in the bud, and not discuss later.

For the Toaster

DO
Look the person you are toasting in the eyes

Take a sip from your glass at the end of your speech

Research, study, and think about the person you are honoring. Ample research often yields a juicy tidbit that can serve as a launching point.

DON'T
Clink your glass with any utensil—damaging your host's fine crystal is a tremendous faux pas!

Slug it like you're in a beer-drinking competition

Try to touch glasses with everyone at the table, as there is a high chance of some seriously misplaced Merlot. Simply raise your glass high.

For the Honoree

DO
Acknowledge the kind words and say thank you

Offer a return toast that thanks everyone for their kind words

Act honored. The most important thing to remember when being on the honored end is to receive the kind words with grace.

DON'T
Drink to yourself (this is like giving yourself a huge pat on the back)

Stand. You should only stand if you opt to give a return toast.

PRACTICE MAKES PERFECT

Even the most eloquent public speakers can find themselves rambling when ill prepared. In the fortunate circumstance that your speech is not entirely impromptu, write it ahead of time. Silly as it sounds, it takes practice to sound spontaneous, so whenever possible, rehearse delivering the toast in advance. Repeat until you can give it fluidly.

If you are the guest of honor you should return the toast. However, do not feel pressure to do so right away. Return toasts don't have to come the moment the first toaster sets down his or her glass. Take some time to ponder your prose and remember that a return toast can be minimal. Even a simple "thank you" will suffice.

DO IT LIKE A STAR

"You should only thank everyone for coming and making it a special evening."　　　　　　　　　　　　　　　　　Dani Janssen

"The best toasts are always from the heart. Speak your mind. Lie in a pinch."　　　　　　　　　　　　　　　　David Arquette

"If it's a dance party, you'd get on the mic and get everyone's attention, then say whatever you have to say. Or scream really loud!"　　　　　　　　　　　　　　　　Sophia Schrager

"Unrehearsed and from the heart. And short."   Peter Som

"One from the heart and spirit . . . I say why I fell for the
person."   Forest Whitaker

TOKEN TOASTS

Every occasion calls for a slightly different toasting protocol. Here
are some toasts that will allow you to navigate each event with ease.
Plus we break down modus operandi for each occasion.

new year's eve

"Here's wishing you more happiness than all my words can tell, not
just alone for New Year's Eve but for all the years as well."

"Here's to the bright new year and a fond farewell to the old."

"Here's to the things that are yet to come and the memories that we
hold."

birthday

"You're not too old when your hair turns gray, you're not too old when
your teeth decay. But you'll know you're awaiting that final sleep
when your mind makes promises your body can't keep."

"May your neighbors respect you, trouble neglect you, the angels protect you, and heaven accept you."

"Here's to Hell! May we have as good a time there as we had getting there."

"Do not resist growing old—many are denied the privilege."

WEDDINGS

Weddings call for a whole separate set of rules. Here's a step-by-step overview that should save you from family extradition, for the time being, anyway.

engagement

"Love does not consist in gazing at each other, but in looking outward together in the same direction."

Antoine de Saint-Exupéry

rehearsal dinner

It is customary that the groom's family hosts this event. The father of the groom should speak first, followed by the best man.

reception

Toasts at the reception should be given in a specific order: best man, maid of honor, groom, bride, father of the bride, groom's father, mother of the bride, and the groom's mother.

WRITER'S BLOCK

On the spot? Cat got your tongue? Crafting a perfect toast is always a challenge. Don't feel overly pressured to create something completely original. In fact, some of the best toasts come from creative combinations of existing materials. When faced with the daunting situation of having to give an impromptu ode, reference some of our "default toasts."

default toasts

"For better, for worse."

"May you live as long as you want and never want as long as you live."
Irish toast

"May all of your joys be pure joys and all of your pain Champagne."

"Drink with impunity—or anyone who happens to invite you!"

"I think that God, in creating man, somewhat overestimated his ability."

"Love doesn't make the world go round, but it does make it interesting."

Mae West

chic tip Worse come to worse? If memorizing a toast proves too difficult, simply raise your glass and express heartfelt thanks for the company of those gathered.

CELEBRITY TOASTS

"I love you, and you are truly someone I can say is a real friend."

Michael Michele

"May the best day of your past be the worst day of your future."

Sarah Michelle Gellar

"Dans les yeux!" (In the eyes!)

Molly Sims

"If you slide down the banister of life, I hope the splinters are kind."

Lara Flynn Boyle

"Bottoms up—there's more where this came from." Billy Bob Thorton

"Here's to love, money, and health."   Michael Kors

"Wishing everyone many blessings from God. To good health and double happiness."   Venus Williams

GIVE MY REGARDS TO HOLLYWOOD

Some of the best lines can be taken right from the Silver Screen. Think back to some of your favorite movies, those great lines that you've never forgotten, and put them to use. Here are some of our favorites.

"After all, tomorrow is another day!"   *Gone With the Wind* (1939)

"There's no place like home."   *The Wizard of Oz* (1939)

"Here's looking at you, kid."   *Casablanca* (1942)

"May the Force be with you."   *Star Wars* (1977)

"Love means never having to say you're sorry."   *Love Story* (1970)

"You had me at hello."   *Jerry Maguire* (1996)

"Mama always said life was like a box of chocolates . . . you never know what you're gonna get."   *Forrest Gump* (1994)

"There's no crying in baseball."   *A League of Their Own* (1992)

"Carpe diem. Seize the day, boys. Make your lives extraordinary."
                                          Dead Poet's Society (1989)

"Never lie, steal, cheat, or drink. But if you must lie, lie in the arms of the one you love. If you must steal, steal away from bad company. If you must cheat, cheat death. And if you must drink, drink in the moments that take your breath away."   *Hitched* (2001)

TIMELESS TOASTS

"Always above you, never below you, always beside you."
                                          Walter Winchell

"When choosing between two evils, I always like to take the one I never tried before."   Mae West

"For better or worse, but never for granted."   Arlene Dahl

"Three be the things I shall never attain, envy, content, and sufficient Champagne."   Dorothy Parker

"The best and most beautiful things in the world cannot be seen, nor even touched, but just felt in the heart."   Helen Keller

take note   In case of emergency, go with this clever line: "I used to know a clever toast, but pshaw! I cannot think of it—So raise your glass to anything. And, bless your souls, I'll drink to it!"

TWELVE GREAT TOASTS

"Peace and plenty for many a Christmas to come."

Traditional Irish toast

"May you live to be a hundred years, with one extra year to repent."

Irish toast

"May you live as long as you love."   Irish toast

"After all these years, I see that I was mistaken about Eve in the beginning; it is better to live outside the Garden with her than inside it without her."   Mark Twain

"There is no greater happiness for a man than approaching a door at the end of a day, knowing someone on the other side of that door is waiting for the sound of his footsteps."   Ronald Reagan

"My wife tells me that if I ever decide to leave, she is coming with me."

Jon Bon Jovi

FOREIGN TOASTS

Foreign in-laws? Festive drinks? Impress your guests with the perfect toast for your signature cocktail, whether it be sake or sangría.

French "À votre santé!" (To your health!)

Italian "Salute!" (Health!) or "Cin cin!" (Cheers!)

British "Cheers!"

Japanese "Kanpai!" (Cheers!)

Swedish "Skål!" (Health!)

Spanish "Salud!" (Health!)

Portuguese "Saúde!" (Health!)

German "Prost!" (Cheers!)

Hebrew "L'chayim!" (To life!)

nine

PRESENT PERFECT

is that for me? why, thank you!

In the entertainment world, gifts come with the territory. And whether you're a host or a guest at a party, you should be well versed in both giving and receiving.

TO GIFT OR NOT TO GIFT

Knowing when to bring a gift is key; there are times when it's ultra-important and times when it's unnecessary. Follow our protocol below, and you'll never wonder again!

- In general, guests should always bring a gift to the host or person of honor. It's especially thoughtful to do so when attending a party in someone's home.

- Large galas, office get-togethers, and parties en masse usually do not require anything cinched with a bow. However, be sure to check the invite carefully, as it may ask for a charitable donation such as toys, clothing, or art supplies.

- Here's the tricky one: If you don't attend, do you need to send a gift? Many people say no, but we firmly believe that you should send a gift either beforehand or as soon as possible after the date, for events such as birthday parties, showers, and so on.

THE BOTTOM DOLLAR: DEALING WITH CHARITY

Charity events can be sticky situations. First off, there's money matters, as in when and how much one should donate. Second, there's that guilt-inducing situation when you don't want to donate time or money to a particular organization. Yes, navigating the charitable waters can be rough, especially when and if your peers are on board and you're the only one running against the current. The following tips are nothing short of a lifesaver.

1. Never attend a charity event without paying. This is not a time to crash or scam a date so you can get that job you've been tracking! Ticket prices are charged as a part of the benefit. The charges help pay for the event so that the proceeds can actually benefit the organization. The only time you should attend without having forked over the cash is as a guest of someone who did pay—for example, often a company will buy a table and then invite attendees.

2. If you are attending a charity event and the contribution is at your discretion, it's entirely up to you to determine the amount. Don't be a tightwad and skip the donation; give what you can afford, that's the bottom line. Every bit counts no matter how little or large.

3. Shopping for a cause is a trendy way to raise money. Hosts will work with a designer or boutique and offer items at a discount with a portion of the cost going toward a selected charity. Simply buy what you can afford. If you don't have a lot of money, then find something small.

4.   Straight up broke? Then don't go. If you're feeling like a charity case yourself, the last thing you should do is put yourself in a position to give money you don't have. If you really want to give something, donate your time and effort. It's just as valuable as money.

5.   Always follow the instructions. If the invite asks you to bring a present like in the case of Toys for Tots, then do so! Don't show up empty-handed.

6.   Find the alternative. If you've been asked to donate money to a cause, think about other things that are within your reach. For example, charity auctions are a great place for people to bid on and win vacations, show walk-ons, pieces of art, couture clothing, and more. Consider your line of work and consider what perks come with the job. For example, Lara and Elizabeth can donate two tickets to a movie premiere and after-party, or an invite to one of the hottest parties around.

7.   Perhaps the hardest encounter is when you have to say no. No one wants to feel uncharitable and saying no is often tantamount to guilt. People in demand and positions of power will often find themselves deluged with requests and not every single one of them can be met. Decline by explaining that you are affiliated with a single cause or that your company has a policy to only donate to children, cancer, homelessness, or whichever founda-tion. For example, Elizabeth dedicates her time to Love Heals. You can preface the no by saying, "That sounds like an amazing cause but we are dedicated to the Breast Cancer Awareness program and that is the charity we support."

ALLISON SAROFIM'S ADVICE ON HOW TO BE THE MOST CHARITABLE PERSON IN TOWN

Allison Sarofim is a contributing editor of *Domino* magazine and the president of 66 Productions. She splits her time between New York and Houston, and gets invited to every party along the way. She's also a huge philanthropist who has hosted charity events for New York City Ballet, Guggenheim Museum, The Public Theatre, The Whitney, and the Martha Ballroom in Martha, Texas. She dishes out her expert advice on how to be the most charitable person in town.

as a chair of a benefit gala, you are expected to sell tickets and tables. how do you go about that?

"You mail invites to your friends with handwritten notes. And a lot of times you buy a table and then invite people. I'm very supportive of my charities whether it is planning the party, attending events, or purchasing a table at an event."

how do you say no to someone who asks you to be on a committee or host something?

"Typically a friend asks me to host, so I'll do it."

what if there's one that you want to be on, but you haven't been asked?

"I would never ask."

TEN GOLDEN RULES OF GIFT GIVING

1. Make it personal! Consider the person who is receiving the gift and choose the gift accordingly. For example, Lara hates receiving liquor as a gift, since her house is overflowing with alcohol from all the parties she's thrown. But she adores getting a bottle of her favorite wine, an '82 Lafite. So take a moment and think about the person you're buying for—what do they love? Is there something they have too much of? If so, avoid! Think about the life they lead and the thing that they really need—and want.

Assortment of host gifts, including TableTopics

Photo credit: Myriam Santos

2. Have as much fun giving as receiving. It's the little touches that spice up even the most standard offerings. Get detail oriented. For example, if you decide vodka is the way to go, create a cool set by including mixers, glassware, and a book of cocktail recipes (you could even go the extra mile and print out your favorite cocktail recipe on a gorgeous piece of paper).

3. Make it a true treat and give something the recipient wouldn't normally buy for themselves.

4. Choose an item that isn't available in the recipient's area. Search for something specific to your city like NYC-based Serendipity's famous frozen hot chocolate or Miami's Joe's Stone Crab Key lime pie.

5. Gift certificates should be thoughtful and tailored to the recipient. If you are not careful, they can come across as impersonal, so think about the recipient and their likes, hobbies, and day-to-day doings. Is there a restaurant, salon, or treatment that they recently mentioned they are dying to try? Maybe it's a session with their trainer or a blowout with their stylist. Just be certain that the gift card is redeemable at their favorite spot, whether it's a boutique, spa, restaurant, or Home Shopping Network—who can't find something they love there?

6. Include a gift receipt so the recipient can return the gift! You may think you know your boss's taste better than anyone but he may already have a stock of crystal candlesticks.

7. In a pinch? Keep a small stash of gifts, boxes, wrapping paper, and ribbon on hand for those impromptu gift-giving moments. Lara keeps Diptyque candles, Ralph Lauren picture frames, and notecards on hand so she's ready to give at a moment's notice.

8. Remember, sometimes the best gifts are the least expensive. As much of a cliché as the saying may be, we truly believe that it is the thought that counts.

9. Presentation is everything! A gift should always be well wrapped and gorgeous; just looking at a pretty package is part of the fun of receiving. Even the most sensational gift can be diluted by a shoddy wrap job. If you're a particularly poor wrapper, fork up the bucks to have it done professionally, and cut the cost by providing the wrapping paper and ribbon.

10. Don't forget the card! One thing that lessens the impact of a gift is the lack of a card. The recipient is left wondering, who is this from? It's great but . . . Get out your pen and sign your name.

IN BLOOM

Sending flowers has its own guidelines. It's more than just grabbing a packaged arrangement from the grocer. We turned to the Birmingham, Alabama, floral guru, Gus Pappas, who owns the state's oldest and largest company, Norton's Florist.

ADVICE FROM GUS PAPPAS

does anyone ever send flowers back?

"Yes, on occasion. And they do it for several reasons. It's a matter of taste and style. Some people like big tacky arrangements, and some like smaller, simpler arrangements. Oftentimes when we're sending a makeup arrangement, the sender will ask our delivery person to stay and wait for a reaction to report back.

"We have delivered flowers where the recipient refuses the arrangement. They will read the card, cuss out the sender, and give them back to our delivery guy. We usually ask if they'd like to just leave them for the girls in the office, but many times they don't even want to see them."

how should one go about sending an anonymous delivery?

"A true reputable and respectable florist tries not to send flowers anonymously. Today, you have to be aware of stalkers and relationships gone bad."

how do you send gifts with flowers?

"We include gifts with flower delivery all the time. Customers will bring in the item, and we will deliver the gift with the flowers. Most commonly we send framed pictures, chocolates, sometimes jewelry, but we pick and choose the jewelry gifts due to the liability involved.

"I know my best clients, and I know what they like and don't like. If someone calls to send one of my clients an arrangement of, say, lilies, and I know that they can't stand lilies, I'll direct the customer to something they actually do like. Everyone wants the person to enjoy the flowers that are sent. Always be sensitive to scent when you are sending an arrangement. Although you may think a flower smells great, the recipient may despise a strongly scented flower.

"Additionally, we will always write the notes for our clients, but we also have a lot of clients that like to fill out their own cards. And sometimes clients are embarrassed by what they are including, so we let them take care of it.

"We once had a man come in on a Friday and order twelve dozen roses. He wanted them delivered by five. I had to ask what the occasion was. His divorce had just finalized and he wanted to get the flowers to his girlfriend's office by five.

"Cash and carry loose roses in a box are always a classy host gift. We'll wrap them in tissue and place them in a box with a beautifully tied ribbon. It's very old school and classic.

"Black roses are bad luck, not to mention poor taste. We get requests for black roses for birthdays. As a rule of thumb, we don't do that. That's one of the oldest tricks in the book as a florist. However, for the opening of *Phantom of the Opera*, we dyed every other stem in black. Hopefully that was only halfway taboo."

It doesn't always have to be a keepsake gift. Consider the context of the event and go with the mood. Singles party? Bring along a gag gift like the decision dice and let the good times roll.

GIFTING DILEMMAS

problem **Millie is pregnant and you are thrilled.** But she's invited you to three different showers, including the super-trendy couple-do next weekend. How do you handle this festival of fêtes?

solution **Having a party-prone group of friends** can lead to gifting dilemmas because there comes a time when enough is enough. If you have a serial soiree-throwin' group of friends, you do not need to give a gift at every party that celebrates the same occasion. Millie will understand if after the first to-do you don't arrive with a slew of ABC blocks and teddy bears! If you absolutely cannot bear the thought of showing up empty-handed, bring a small token with you the day of the event.

problem **Oh no! You were so in love,** until you found out your husband-to-be is the farthest thing from the man of your dreams. Making matters worse, you have piles and piles of gifts from your engagement party, bridal shower, and even early bird wedding gifts.

solution **Yes, you have to give back every single gift.** No, you can't keep them—even if you feel like you deserve to from putting up with all the stress of calling off your big day. Whether the ending was traumatic, amicable, or even if you got stood up at the altar, all the pretty packages go back to the givers. And that includes the engagement ring. Hand it over, honey!

problem **Suzie has searched high and low for the perfect gift** for her best friend's thirtieth birthday. Now the birthday girl's party is minutes away, and it looks like Suzie is going to arrive empty-handed. What to do?

solution **There are so many reasons why a present is belated.** Perhaps it never arrived, it's on back order, or the perfect present just hasn't appeared. Instead of showing up with nada, make a sweet birthday card and pair it with a thoughtful token. Let her know there is more to come, you've been searching high and low!

problem **It's time for Ryan's annual birthday shindig,** but you're headed out of town that weekend. Can you skip out on a gift, just this once?

solution **No! You don't have to break the bank,** but the nice (and appropriate) thing to do is send a gift ahead of time. Or, if you'll be spending your weekend in a place where you can find something Ryan would just love, love, love, pick his birthday present up on your travels.

problem **Richard is throwing a huge bash at a nightclub** for two hundred of his nearest and dearest to celebrate his twenty-ninth birthday. Do you bring a gift?

solution **Of course!** It's best to send the gift before or after his brouhaha, as with this kind of scene going down, it's likely he will misplace your thoughtful gesture, so send it, with a card, naturally, the day before or day after.

BETTER LATE THAN NEVER!

There are degrees of tardiness on the gift-giving continuum, but the bottom line states it is never too late to send a gift; we believe that belated is always better than never. In an ideal world you should present your gift at the time of the event or, if it is more convenient, ahead of time.

However, if you are delayed by laziness, forgetfulness, or any such sin, acknowledge the delay in an accompanying card (self-deprecation is highly encouraged) and send as soon as possible. If you have entered the realm of embarrassingly late, take time beforehand to check in with the birthday girl, mama-to-be, etc., by phone and grovel. Don't buffer your tardiness with a drawn-out excuse. The perfect pretext is as easy as "It took me so long to find the perfect gift!" You'll be forgiven instantly!

take note

People are often conflicted about giving money versus a gift. Generally, we are not fans of the cash-stuffed envelope. However, on some occasions it is absolutely the preferred present, like at a graduation or wedding. If you opt to go green, don't just scrawl out a check and shove it in an envelope. Give the gift a personal touch. Put the money in a novelty piggy bank that says something clever: "Vacation Fund," "Retirement Fund," "Rainy Day," "Botox Bank," or "Shopping Therapy."

chic tip   Gift registry is there for a reason, so use it! While we are the number one fans of the creative gift, in this case, the recipient has picked these items for a reason: they want it! Be inventive with the selection by spicing it up with a personal touch.

Get Personal

We love anything monogrammed, whether it be a wine stopper, doormat, or stationery.

If you opt to monogram something, make sure to employ the proper design. For a couple, e.g., John and Mary Smith, use the following format: JSM. For an individual, John Edward Smith, use first and last or first, middle, and last initials: JS or JES.

FIVE CUSTOM-CRAFTED GIFTS

1. IPOD WITH PLAYLIST It's the mix tape for the new millennium. Making a playlist is super easy, and a great way to bring back a memory or say something special.

2. CUSTOM-MIXED CD Don't have the moolah to spring for an iPod? Go old-school and create a cool CD.

3. PERSONALIZED STATIONERY No one can ever have

enough notecards and pads of paper; it's always useful. Some of our favorites are Cartier, Smythson, or go to a place like Wren Press and create something unique.

4. ZAZZLE STAMPS/CUSTOM POSTAGE Such a cute idea. Simply pick out a favorite photo or image, like that silly prom picture of you and your best friend from ten years ago, and mail it in to create a custom stamp. Check out the United States Post Office and www.zazzle.com for more info.

5. PHOTO ALBUM This is such a fantastic gift that doesn't cost a lot. You can create a book of photos using online resources such as Snapfish, iPhoto, Hallmark, Kodak, and more. Or if you're armed with a disc full of images, you can also head to the photo department of Target or Best Buy and print out a bunch of your favorite snapshots. Buy a sweet photo album (any size will do) with acid-free paper (so it'll last forever) and create a book full of memories. Lara's favorite photo album place is Ronnie Gousman, which carries gorgeous leather-bound books that you'll want to keep forever.

FIVE GIFTS THAT KEEP ON GIVING

1. MAGAZINE OR NEWSPAPER SUBSCRIPTIONS Think of the recipient's hobbies and go for it. For example, a pal consumed with shopping will love *Vogue, W,* or *Lucky* magazine. A foodie will go head over heels for *Bon Appétit, Food and Wine,*

or *Gourmet*, and no guy would say no to *Sports Illustrated, or The Wall Street Journal.*

2. MONTHLY FLORAL DELIVERY Such a sensational gift for the person who has everything. Keep in mind the flowers they love—or hate—and make note when ordering.

3. WATER DELIVERY Could there be anything better for that workout-charged friend?

4. PHOTO PRINTER Such a great gift for new parents! Now they can print out all of those adorable, cute shots of their wee ones.

5. LOTTERY TICKET Need we say more? And no, you don't get a cut if millions are won.

FIVE NOVELTIES

1. FIRST-EDITION BOOKS One of Lara's all-time favorite gifts is her set of first-edition Nancy Drew books, given to her by Jay Penske, who owns a first-edition bookstore called Dragon Books. This is a wonderful idea for a writer or avid reader.

2. RESTAURANT COOKBOOKS PAIRED WITH FAMOUS CHEF'S SAUCES Adding the chef's sauces or the ingredients for one of your favorite dishes makes this a wonderful gift. If you go with ingredients, consider those that can be frozen or are

long lasting so the goods don't go to waste. Lara's favorite cookbooks include *Hollywood Dish* by Akasha Richmond, any of Ina Garten's Barefoot Contessa cookbooks, *The Balthazar Cookbook* by Keith McNally, and others. *Nobu* by Nobu Matsuhisa, *The Craft of Cooking* by Tom Colicchio, Mario Batali's *Simple Italian good,* and Giada De Laurentiis's *Everyday Italian,* and no kitchen should be without *Joy of Cooking.*

3. TABLE TOPICS One of our favorite party add-ons, this question 'n' answer game comes in a beautiful Lucite box filled with conversation-starting questions.

4. MOVIE NIGHT KIT Group together a set of classic DVDs, fresh popcorn, and theater-style candy (think Red Vines and Milk Duds) in a great big bowl.

5. OLD SCHOOL GAMES Think Monopoly, Twister, and more. This is a fun gift to bring to a small gathering of friends because you can put it to use right away!

chic tip

A great gift is to send a host something that they can't get in their home town. Lara loves to send New York City's H&H Bagels or Kansas City barbecue from Fiorella's Jack Stack. A hangover kit makes a great gift for your host. Contents: all the fixins' for a Bloody Mary, and plenty of Advil, water, and Emergen-C.

Other Great Gifts

Here are more creative ideas for gift-giving. Let our list inspire you to think out of the box.

VISIT TO A SALON A gift certificate to a favorite stylist will always be appreciated. Whether it's to a personal stylist or a hot new salon where everyone's dying to get a trim, our favorites include Frederic Fekkai, Oribe, John Barrett, the Four Seasons, Cornelia Day Spa, or anywhere equally famous in your home town. Make it an extra special gift by sending it beforehand so the host can indulge the day of!

PRIVATE TRAINING The workout warrior will thank you! Especially since they can sweat out all the stress from party planning.

RECORD STORE With a gift certificate, the music lover will be in heaven stocking up on great new CDs or records for their next bash.

PICTURE FRAME You can't go wrong! Personalize it by putting in a photo from the party or one of you and the host out on the town.

MONOGRAM IT! Anything monogrammed, whether it's stationery, hand towels, bar glasses, coasters, napkins, or picture frames.

CANDLES It's the must-have for every host and no one can ever have enough. Lara and Elizabeth's favorites are Diptyque and Harry Slatkin. You can also dip into the new scent trend and hand over incense or aroma sticks, which come in every scent imaginable.

NOTEBOOKS, CALENDARS, AND DIARIES Smythson of Bond Street makes the best gifts of this type. We especially adore their travel books for the blonde, brunette, and redhead.

TIPS FOR GIVING AND RECEIVING

for the guest

As we stated about a thousand times, but we'll say it again just in case you missed it, guests should always bring a gift to their host. Host gifts should be thoughtful, personal, and very low maintenance. Contrary to popular belief, we suggest avoiding the usual go-tos of flowers or food (excluding, of course, a box of fine chocolates). Let's be honest, however beautiful the bouquet, your host doesn't want to have to scramble for a suitable vase in the middle of dinner preparations or greeting guests. Should you opt for flowers, go for a potted plant (we love orchids) or send an arrangement the following day.

If you bring a dish of food, be realistic and do not expect the host to serve your dish at the party—even if you are a gourmet chef! It is likely that a meticulously crafted bill of fare is already in place and your dish—however yummy—may clash. The same goes for flowers and alcohol of any kind. The best thing to do is either send these items ahead of time or clear it with the host beforehand. Why? Because you want to make sure that the food is wanted, needed, and goes with the planned menu, and that the florals match her planned décor.

for the host

The most important part of present protocol is receiving a gift with grace. Surely we don't have to tell you this, but never say anything negative or disapproving. And along the same lines, don't be overly enthusiastic, as you may come across phony.

Be selective with your adjectives—words like "unique" or "original" can be interpreted as negative. Best bet? Avoid describing the gift at all. Instead, smile and say, "This is so thoughtful, thank you."

Never make a comment about returning or exchanging a gift or ask for the receipt. And don't ever inquire about how much a gift costs. But you knew that, right? Right!

When Regifting Goes Good

Normally, regifting is a no-no. But there are times when it's not only acceptable, but incredibly thoughtful. Namely, when it's something that you have that someone admires, adores, and loves, but the item is no longer available. For example, Michael Michele loved Lara's big, fluffy, soft cotton robe. She searched high and low, tried to find something similar to no avail. Finally, she took the robe to the dry cleaner, bought a beautiful box, and wrote a simple, funny card to accompany her robe. You can do the same with a dress, jewelry, vintage bag, or shoes—anything that is one of a kind!

WHAT'S THE BEST GIFT YOU HAVE BEEN GIVEN AS A HOST?

Unique, thoughtful gifts are never forgotten. Here are some of the best ones!

"A European DJ."   Hugh Jackman

"A dear friend prepared extraordinary hors d'oeurves for my cocktail party as my gift."   Michael Michele

"A three-tiered cake stand, monogrammed boxed matches, and monogrammed paper napkins."   Allison Sarofim

WHAT WAS THE BEST GIFT YOU EVER GAVE TO A HOST?

Still at a loss for a great gift? Take inspiration from this list of ideas.

"Appetizers by Chef Bill Granger."   Hugh Jackman

"Monogrammed Frette sheets, and I love the chic Vosges chocolate because it is beautifully wrapped. I like to go to a flea market and find an old vase and put flowers in it, and I like funny but inexpensive gifts. I'm a big fan of witty and well-packaged gifts."   Allison Sarofim

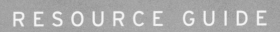

RESOURCE GUIDE

One. PARTY PLANNING 101

Restaurants are a great place to host a party.

Mr. Chow
344 N. Camden Dr
Beverly Hills, CA 90210
310.278.9911
www.mrchow.com
This chic, upscale Chinese eatery is a favorite hangout for celebrities and the ultimate see-and-be-seen spot. Locations also in New York, London, and Miami.

Hamburger Hamlet
9201 Sunset Blvd
West Hollywood, CA 90069
310.278.4924
This LA institution, where the burger is the main fare, has been serving up traditional American fare since 1950. Nine locations in Los Angeles.

Cipriani's
110 East 42nd St
New York, NY 10017
Serves up legendary Italian fare straight from Harry's Bar in Venice, Italy. Other locations in New York, Hong Kong, London, Italy, and Argentina.

Dan Tana's
9071 Santa Monica Blvd
West Hollywood, CA 90069
310.275.9444
www.dantanasrestaurant.com
Taking a cue from the red-sauced Italian joints of yore, this celeb-loved hangout is casual, unpretentious, and perfect for any party.

Pink Taco
10250 Santa Monica Blvd
Los Angeles, CA 90067
310.789.1000
www.pinktaco.com
Tricked out with cool, kitschy décor, Harry Morton's restaurant serves up
tasty Mexican food in a festive setting. Other locations also in Phoenix and
Las Vegas.

Jumeirah Essex House
160 Central Park West
New York, NY 10019
212.247.0300
www.jumeirahessexhouse.com
This famous Art Deco hotel serves up some of the finest afternoon tea in
New York.

Koi
730 North La Cienega Blvd
Los Angeles, CA 90069
310.659.9449
www.koirestaurant.com
Sushi and signature menu items like spicy tuna on crispy rice make this a
fabulous spot to order up a ton of bite-size items to share. Other locations
include New York and Las Vegas.

Il Sole
8741 Sunset Blvd
West Hollywood, CA 90069
310.657.1182
Delicious Italian fare served up in a romantic, yet bustling spot. Private
dining room is available for up to thirty-five as is private catering.
Serendipity 3

225 East 60th St
New York, NY 10022
212.838.3531
www.serendipity3.com
Sweet tooths need look no farther than this decadent spot featuring ice cream and frozen delights that even Willy Wonka couldn't have dreamed up.

Nobu
www.noburestaurants.com
Some of the best sushi in the world is found here. Locations in Malibu, New York City, Hawaii, Dallas, Miami Beach, London, Milan, Melbourne, Hong Kong, Toyko.

Hotel Bel-Air
701 Stone Canyon Rd
Los Angeles, CA 90077
310.472.1211
www.hotelbelair.com
This five-star hotel situated in the heart of Bel-Air boasts one of the most amazing settings for an event with its wine terrace, banquet rooms, and gardens.

Wolfgang Puck
www.wolfgangpuck.com
There's a taste for everyone with Wolfgang Puck restaurants, including Spago, Chinois, Cut, Postrio, The Source, Trattoria del Lupo, Wolfgang Puck American Grille, Wolfgang Puck Bar and Grille, 2021, PUCK's, Vert, Red Seven, Wolfgang Puck Gourmet Express, and Wolfgang Puck Café.

N9NE Steakhouse at Palms Casino Resort
4321 West Flamingo Rd

Las Vegas, NV 89103
702.933.9900
www.palms.com

Nove Italiano at Palms Casino Resort
4321 West Flamingo Rd
Las Vegas, NV 89103
702.933.9900
www.palms.com

Alize at Palms Casino Resort
4321 West Flamingo Rd
Las Vegas, NV 89103
702.933.9900
www.palms.com

The Polo Lounge at the Beverly Hills Hotel
9641 Sunset Blvd
Beverly Hills, CA 90210
310.276.2251
www.thebeverlyhillshotel.com

Four. MIND YOUR P'S & Q'S

Paper Source
www.paper-source.com
Paper Source is a chic place to pick out your invitations and thank-you notes.

Cartier Stationery
www.cartier.com

GREAT PRINTER
Steve from Alpine Creative Group
www.alpinecreativegroup.com

GREAT CALLIGRAPHERS
Bernard Maisner
www.bernardmaisner.com

Stephanie Barba
www.stephaniebarba.com

Peter Som
www.petersom.com
Not only does Peter Som offers the best fashion dos and don'ts, he also has
an amazing collection perfect for a guest or hostess.

Catherine Malandrino
www.catherinemalandrino.com
Aside from lending her priceless fashion advice, Catherine Malandrino
produces styles perfect for the a swankiest of sources.

Five. GUESTLY MANNERS

Renowned photographers reveal their best secrets to looking great in every
photograph.

Patrick McMullan Company
www.patrickmcmullan.com

Jeff Vespa
www.jeffvespa.com

Myriam Santos-Kayda
www.myriamsantoskayda.com

Tierney Gearon
www.tierneygearon.com

Seven. COCKTAIL CONDUCT

Our friends at Veuve Clicquot Champagne offer the proper etiquette to toast
with the best Champagne.

Veuve Clicquot
www.veuve-clicquot.com

Grey Goose Vodka
www.greygoose.com

Nine. PRESENT PERFECT

Everyone loves a gift. Here are some of our favorites to give and receive.

Joe's Stone Crab (gift certificate)
11 Washington Ave
Miami, FL 33139
305.673.0365
www.joesstonecrab.com

Diptyque (candles)
www.diptyqueparis.com

Home Shopping Network
www.hsn.com

Ralph Lauren (frames)
www.RalphLauren.com

Zazzle (stamps)
www.zazzle.com

Dragon Books 1st Edition Bookstore
2954 Beverly Glen Circle
Bel-Air, CA 90077
310.441.8545
www.dragonbooks.com

iPod/Apple
www.Apple.com

Ronnie Gousman
www.oakknollbooks.com

Vivre
www.vivre.com
Unique gifts from international designers and luxury brands for women, men, kids, and the home.

Kitson
116 North Robertson Blvd
Suite C

Los Angeles, CA 90048
310.289.4975
www.shopkitson.com

ADDITIONAL RESOURCES

Magazine and Newspaper Subscriptions

Vogue magazine
W magazine
Lucky magazine
Bon Appétit magazine
The Wall Street Journal
Food and Wine magazine
Gourmet magazine
Domino magazine
Vanity Fair magazine
The New York Times
New York Post

Old School Games

Monopoly
www.Monopoly.com

Twister
www.twister.com

Favorite Cookbooks

Keith McNally, Riad Nasr, and Lee Hanson, *The Balthazar Cookbook.*
   Clarkson Potter.

Ina Garten, *Barefoot Contessa Family Style.* Clarkson Potter.

Mario Batali, *Simple Italian Food.* Random House.

Tom Colicchio, *Craft of Cooking.* Clarkson Potter.

Jennifer Appel and Allysa Toyer, *The Magnolia Bakery Cookbook.* Simon & Schuster.

Arrigo Cipriani and Harry Cipriani, *The Harry's Bar Cookbook.* Bantam Books.

Brigit Légere Binns, *The Palm Restaurant Cookbook.* Running Press.

Nobu Matsuhisa, *Nobu: The Cookbook.* Kodansha, America.

Daniel Boulud and Peter Kaminsky, *Chef Daniel Boulud: Cooking in New York City.* Assouline.

Florist

Norton's Florist
www.nortonsflorist.com

ACKNOWLEDGMENTS

Lara and Elizabeth would like to thank . . .

Dan Strone, our great book agent at Trident Media.

Our amazing team at Harrison & Shriftman, especially Kim Pappas, Sarah Imparato, Jennifer Styles, and our two great interns who helped with so much research, Caitlyn Crisp and Lauren Tejeda.

John Palermo, Erin Franklin, Kristin Scott, Alletta Kriak, Matt Minnis, Andrea Collins, Elana Posner, Rochelle Lecavalier, Rob Hilburger, and Jonathan Shriftman.

Lauren Malone, Carolyn Aker of Table Topics, Matt Ninnis, Kelli Delaney, Il Sole's Andy Hewitt and Doug Major, Nobu's Erica Matsunaga, Serendipity's Stephen Bruce, Jumeirah Essex House's Christian Gradnitzer, Spago's Wolfgang Puck, Koi's Corinne Lazarz, Kerry Simon at Palms Place, and The Bel-Air Hotel's Michael Manoocheri for their tips on making dinner reservations.

Noah Tepperberg, Andrew Goldberg, and Rich Thomas for their insight on nightclub etiquette.

Jeff Vespa and WireImage, Myriam Santos-Kayda, Patrick McMullan, and Tierney Gearon for their tips how to pose for a photo.

All the photographers that contributed to the book, John Shearer, Denise Truscello, and Myriam Santos-Kayda.

David Arquette, Stephen Dorff, Gigi Grazer, Hugh Jackman, Dani Janssen, Michael Michele, Harry Morton, Sophia and Ava Schrager, Molly Sims, Bruce Taylor, Playboy's Mary O'Connor, Vanna White, Gus Pappas, and Serena Williams for their wonderful tips on entertaining.

Sarah Michelle Gellar, Venus Williams, Forest Whitaker, and Michael Kors, and Veuve Clicquot for their tips on how to make a toast.

Catherine Malandrino and Peter Som for their tips on what to wear.

Thank you to our parents for their love and inspiration.

ABOUT THE AUTHORS

Lara Shriftman and Elizabeth Harrison are the principals at the high-profile public relations, special events, and marketing firm Harrison & Shriftman, with offices in New York, Los Angeles, and Miami. Famous for branding companies, marketing, and generating A-list publicity, their special events division has produced many highly publicized events, including movie premieres for *Charlie's Angels, Bridget Jones Diary,* and *Legally Blonde*; store openings for Michael Kors, Scoop, and Hogan; charity events for Love Heals, ABT, and Toys for Tots; fashion shows for Catherine Malandrino, Oscar de la Renta, Jill Stuart, and Lacoste; product launches for BlackBerry, Cartier, Calvin Klein, Juicy Couture, and Motorola; and birthday bashes for Billy Bob Thornton, Rachel Hunter, Luke Wilson, Reggie Miller, Serena Williams, Stevie Wonder, and more.

After the release of their books *Party Confidential, Fête Accompli!: The Ultimate Guide to Creative Entertaining* and *Fête Accompli! Workbook: The Ultimate Party Planning Guide,* Lara and Elizabeth were touted as the experts in party planning by magazines that include *Vanity Fair, Glamour, Seventeen,* and *Departures,* as well as television shows such as *Extra TV* and *E! News*. In addition, they have a line of party necessities (glassware, vases, and more) entitled Party Confidential with Home Shopping Network.

Lara Morgenson is the executive editor of *LA Confidential,* a Los Angeles–based luxury lifestyle magazine that covers the best that the city has to offer in the worlds of fashion, beauty, business, dining, entertainment, interior design, nightlife, philanthropy, and travel. Previously, she created and wrote the A-list column, "Hollywood Party Girl," on E! Online. She co-wrote *Party Confidential* and has been published in *Los Angeles* magazine, *Angeleno,* and various other publications.

Elizabeth Keen, a graduate of the University of Southern California, is a valued member of the Harrison & Shriftman team. She works tirelessly with H & S's high-profile clients and accounts, including Il Sole, BlackBerry, Koi, Members Only, and Palms Casino Resort. In addition, she oversees editorial photo shoots and is a key player in product development and coordinating brand launch parties. Keen plays an integral role in building the Party Confidential brand.